Her Island:
The Story of Quetico's Longest Serving Interior Ranger

Joe Friedrichs

10,000 Lakes Publishing

Janice Matichuk
July 24, 1954–August 5, 2020

To all those fighting to protect clean water.
-Joe

Table of Contents

Foreword
by Ingela Puddicombe

I'm sitting along the shores of French lake, at the Dawson Trail entry point to Quetico Provincial Park. I'm in a fantastic little single-room cabin with no running water or plumbing. There are large windows on each wall. The cabin, known as "The Artist's Retreat," is the only place I can think of that would be nearly as meaningful as far as a setting to write these words, at least when compared to the island at Cache Bay.

When Joe Friedrichs, the author of this book, was finally able to pin me down and get my bits for the project, I was not terribly easy to deal with or helpful about our time at Cache Bay. I've long battled our time there in my mind. So when he asked me to write this, I was surprised, but I am so grateful for the opportunity to do so.

I never imagined that this book was going to come out after our mom died. In fall 2019, our biggest crisis was Mom's finger and Joe being able to get what he needed for this book to become a reality. Now that Mom has passed away, if ever there was time to write this book and get it finished, Joe nailed it, like to the minute. That the book comes out the year Mom died is surreal to me as I put these words down on paper.

Looking back, nothing can compare to the lives we lived during our summers on the island at Cache Bay. It is not the most remote or isolated location a ranger or other worker is posted at in the world. It's neither the most prestigious nor the most famous. All the same, life there certainly was, and still is incredibly unique and dreamed of in the minds of many. It remains so in my own mind.

With Mom's passing, we can finally let out a few of the tales we've been holding all these years. Stories like Mom riding on a homemade disc we rigged out of an old park display of sorts that we would tug behind a motorboat. Think of a disc you ride going down a sledding hill and you are on the right track. On nights when we were sure that no campers were in the bay, the fun would begin. I recall Dad driving the boat, with Mom on the disc being pulled behind. I remember laughing under the stars as she did complete 360s, wild jumps, crossed over the wake from one side to another and back again. At times like these, she had that devilish smile and unwavering confidence surrounding her. This was when the Matichuk in her really showed, all across her grinning face that said without words: "I dare you to be this good."

In recent years and now since Mom has passed, I've heard a lot of sentiments along the lines of "Cache Bay won't be Cache Bay without Janice." Perhaps it's true, in part. The thing to remember is that Mom was not the first ranger or the last one to look over Cache Bay. She is indeed the longest serving ranger and undeniably was a force of good to be reckoned with. The island, Quetico, and the world will be lucky to see the likes of someone like her again. However, over all the years, Mom was just one of the incredible rangers stationed at this post. Mom always wanted us to remember that. The first Cache Bay ranger, Art Madsen, was as an accomplished and incredible person. Largely because of their shared understanding of Cache Bay and the community on Sag Lake, Art was a dear friend to Mom and our family. Art's family remains at his homestead on Sag to this day. Tragically, many forget about those who were here before these wilds had the name "Quetico." From Chief Blackstone to other Indigenous families who called this area home, the history here is rich with connection to the land. We must also remember the Powell family, some of whom still live on Sag seasonally and know every inch and story of the area.

One can't begin to explain why Mom loved Cache Bay the way she did without mentioning the Gunflint Trail, Grand Marais, and the many residents who she loved dearly. What Mom gave to Cache Bay, the land and water, and the paddling community gave back. However, there was another side to the job. It was sometimes sad, lonely, and occasionally broken. It brings me to tears just trying to write about it. Mom was so dedicated to her job that it often consumed her. She identified so much by her role as the Cache Bay ranger that she could get lost in it, falling into depression in the winter when she was away from the island.

As Mom loved the job so much, we knew she might never step away or retire. One of the last things I said to her was, "The universe knew you were never going to retire, Mom, so it's retiring you." She agreed with a half-smile and nod as she was in her last days and not able to communicate.

But what is the island now? How will it look when we come around the corner of Cache Point, or when it comes into sight below us when we fly in? What is there waiting for us now? Not Mom, who many simply knew as Ranger Janice. That much we know. The island is still here, though, and there's comfort in that. So too are Mom's stories. It's just a new chapter.

Joe, whatever made you start this project, thank you so very kindly. It is truly incredible how this lined up. It cannot be a coincidence. On behalf of my brother and me, we are forever in your debt.

~Ingela Puddicombe, Janice Matichuk's daughter

The eternal equilibrium of things is great, and the eternal overthrow of things is great, and there is another paradox.

Great is life ... and real and mystical, wherever and whoever.

Great is death . . . Sure as life holds all parts together, death holds all parts together;

Sure as the stars return again after they merge in the light, death is great as life.

- Walt Whitman

Publisher's Note

Our goal was to keep as many of the direct quotes in this book as untouched as possible. Due to the timing of Janice Matichuk's passing, some of these quotes from the author's interviews are phrased as though she is still with us. While this is tragically no longer the case, through her actions, friendships, and these words, her legacy lives on.

In Janice's honor, 10,000 Lakes Publishing will donate 10% of profits from *Her Island* to nonprofit clean water advocates.

Chapter One
Dark Skies Over the Boundary Waters

On a brisk morning during the first week of June 2000, Quetico Park Ranger Janice Matichuk paused to take an especially long sip from her steaming mug of dark roast coffee. It was the start of a new day for the venerable park ranger, and for the several hundred canoeists currently camping inside the park. The Cache Bay Ranger Station on Saganaga Lake—where Matichuk sipped her coffee—serves as the southeastern entrance to the 1.2 million-acre Quetico Provincial Park. Within eyesight of the island-outpost on Saganaga Lake is the international border line separating Canada and the United States on Saganaga Lake.

Nearly 14,000 acres in size, Sag, as it's commonly called by the more familiar, is surrounded by the Boundary Waters Canoe Area Wilderness in the States to the south, and by Quetico and La Verendrye Provincial Parks in Canada to the north and east. It is a deep, pure, iron-tinged body of water made up of many dozens of islands, channels, bays, peninsulas, and reefs. A magnet for harsh weather, Sag sits locked in ice for about half of the year. It is a cold, unforgiving body of water surrounded by chiseled granite and towering pines. Of the more than 1,000 lakes in the BWCA and another 2,000 in Quetico, Sag is among the deepest and largest of them all.

After a string of pleasant days and nights, today's forecast called for strong winds and rain. Following another sip of coffee, Matichuk called in to park headquarters on an old-school CB radio. She reported that she had multiple permits to issue before the day's end, and that she hoped to get some work done on the island's lone latrine before the rain swept through.

This island and the 800-square-foot cabin provided modest accommodations for Matichuk, the longest serving ranger in the history of Quetico Park, for more than three decades. She raised a family here, witnessed tragedies, laughed until she cried, watched people grow into adulthood, and grew deeply connected to the natural world surrounding her. In other words, on this tiny island, Matichuk experienced everything life in the *real world* can offer a human being. Within that truth and life experience, Matichuk had come to understand that here—Mother Nature reigns supreme.

After a rather routine day, Matichuk settled in to the late afternoon ease of life on the remote island. The wind and rain common on these giant border lakes arrived as predicted and Matichuk had early dinner on her mind. While grabbing additional pieces of fuel—split birch—to bring inside for the evening fire, Matichuk noticed something out of place.

This happens from time to time after spending years in a more natural silence, where motors are banned and human activity is sparse. Anything out of the ordinary—sight, smell, sound, or mere feeling—is instantly recognizable to Matichuk. The disturbances, when audible, often come from an animal—an eagle, wolf, or loon.

On this June afternoon, it was not the howl of a wolf that stopped her. This particular sound came from something else. With the branches of massive red pines rustling in the building wind, Matichuk stood still and waited. It repeated. The sound traveled across the water and seemed to settle on her island. Something was out there, and she knew it was wrong.

It had been nearing 4 p.m. when Matichuk heard the noise. In Quetico, strange sounds have the power to transform more than the moment. They change lives. This sound, a mere whimper on the horizon, held that type of power.

"You get to know the island. You know what fits and what doesn't," said Matichuk, nineteen years later. "Even though this sound was so faint, it just didn't belong, and I could feel something was off."

She heard it again, louder this time. Standing on the northeast side of her small cabin, Matichuk darted inside to grab her raingear. As Sag often does, the fierce weather intensified by the second. Matichuk's young son, Leif, was inside tending to the cabin's wood-burning stove, having sought shelter from the storm.

"Were you outside yelling just a minute ago?" Matichuk asked her son.

Leif shook his head slowly from left to right.

"Did you hear a voice?" Janice asked.

"No."

Leif, who was eleven at the time, said he'd been inside for at least thirty minutes. He hadn't heard anything unusual. Both Janice and Leif shifted their attention to the expansive south-facing windows that ran the length of the wall, facing toward the southern entrance to Cache Bay. Without another word, Janice rushed to her bedroom, pulled on her rain pants, then grabbed the jacket and life preserver from a hook near the office desk, darting out of the front entrance.

Something was amiss on the water. Her instincts powered her steps.

"I just had an intuition that something was wrong," Matichuk said. "I thought people were out there. I don't know why."

Normally agile and confident as she moved about the island, at that time, Matichuk was having to mind a heavy, awkward cast covering her left foot. She'd broken a bone in her foot several weeks before and it now forced her to move that much more intentionally. To keep the cast dry, Matichuk had haphazardly wrapped two bright yellow garbage bags around her foot, using duct tape to seal the bags tightly to her leg.

The park service kept a small motorboat at the dock down the hill below the ranger station. Janice hobbled down it toward the boat, moving as quickly as possible. Still not knowing for sure if anything or anyone needed her help, Janice carefully stepped from the dock to the boat. She then ripped a weathered 20-horse four-stroke motor to life, her propulsion affixed to the stern, or back, of the boat. It took three pulls on its lawnmower-style starter-cord for the engine to sputter from slumber. Finally, it hummed a steady hymn.

The bottom of the aluminum boat had several inches of water sloshing about, the result of a heavy rain from the ongoing storm. Frantically, Matichuk bailed the water using an old tin one-gallon can.

The wind continued to rip across the water, waves crashing against the dock with the steadiness of drummers in a marching band. Some of the waves sent the idling boat crashing into its moorings.

"I still didn't know if anyone was out there," Matichuk said. "With those conditions, normally, I would never go out on the water, even in the motorboat."

With enough water emptied from the bottom of the boat, Janice freed the craft from the dock, undoing the knots on two weathered ropes, one near the bow, the other near the stern. She threw the engine into gear and the boat bobbed away from the dock. Janice inhaled slowly while getting her bearings. Her eyes swept across the water and saw a sea of violent waves. She twisted the engine's throttle and the boat pushed headlong into the tempest.

Several hours before Matichuk heard the faint cry carry across Cache Bay to her island, Mark Hargis nonchalantly stuffed his sleeping bag and other gear into a large, traditional gear bag known as a Duluth Pack. A canvas bag and predecessor to the type of backpack one would use on extended hiking trips through mountainous terrain, a Duluth Pack is typically wider and shorter than a typical hiking backpack. In every sense, they're built for canoe country traveling.

Hargis was among five others who'd been camping, fishing, and paddling together in Quetico for the past week. Others along for the journey included Mark's brother Peter, his cousins Scott Black and Rob Anderson, and his uncle Jeff Hargis. Rounding out the party was Mark's friend, Tom Ackerman.

Stocky, with brown hair and built like somebody who might be a collegiate wrestler, this was Ackerman's first trip to the Boundary Waters region. Albeit somewhat shifty in the canoe to start the expedition, Ackerman had settled in during the past seventy-two hours and was now consistently catching walleye, sharing stories around the nightly campfire, and moving in unison with the rest of the group. Fresh off his junior year of college at the University of Montana, Ackerman was glad to be back in Minnesota for a vacation with his friends. Returning to Minnesota also provided an opportunity for Ackerman to spend time with his father, who lived in the Twin Cities area, about five hours south of the

Boundary Waters. Already planning beyond graduation, Ackerman hoped to pursue a master's degree in business at the University of Minnesota once he was finished at school in Missoula that spring.

Ackerman was born in Minnesota but spent most of his childhood near Billings in Montana. After completing his sophomore year at Billings West High School, the family returned to Minnesota, where Ackerman spent his final two years of high school in Woodbury. It was here that Ackerman and Hargis met and quickly formed a strong friendship. Both were standout athletes on the high school football and baseball teams. Outside of school, Ackerman's family had a pool in their backyard and, living in the same neighborhood, swimming was a convenient and frequent summertime activity for the duo.

Unlike Ackerman, Hargis was an experienced canoeist prior to their journey. He'd paddled across many Boundary Waters lakes with friends and family during the first twenty-one years of his life. It was this experience that made him the de facto leader of the expedition. From the planning stages, to the person who called many of the shots along the way once their paddles hit the water, Hargis embraced the role.

Until now, for each day on the water and at multiple camps along the way, every element of the journey had been ideal. The fishing was solid, with northern pike and prized walleye commonplace at the end of their lines. They felt stable enough that by the second day of the trip, no one in the group wore a life jacket while in their canoes.

The group spent most of their trip on Kawnipi Lake. Known to be a fishing paradise, the lake sits fifteen miles and nine portages north of Cache Bay. On the night of May 31, the group made a consensus decision to break camp and head back to Tuscarora Lodge & Outfitters on the Gunflint Trail the following morning. They were heading in early, but the threat of bad weather in the forecast made the decision easier to make. The staff at Tuscarora had rented the six ambitious paddlers three aluminum canoes and gave them a motorized transport to American Point on Sag to start the trip. This is common among parties entering through Cache Bay, as it gets canoeists deeper into the wilderness more quickly, beyond a long channel and then the expansive heart of Sag.

"Once the weather switched up, we were ready for a warm meal and a bed off the ground," Hargis said.

Leaving their quiet solitude on Kawnipi Lake, the group spent their final night in Quetico camped just above a beautiful stretch of water known as the Falls Chain. Much of the water in canoe country is connected by moving water, everything from small inlet creeks to powerful and roaring stretches of whitewater. Tranquil as it is, the Falls Chain is also a dangerous setting and essentially impossible to paddle. Matichuk routinely went over maps, corrected portages, and educated paddlers so that they had a full understanding and respect for that passage. She often showed incoming paddlers a photograph she took of a canoe that went down the falls and became wrapped around a boulder in the turgid water. The canoe still rests in this flow, now surrounded by logs and other debris.

To navigate the falls, canoeists must portage around each separate segment of the most intense flow areas, with actual waterfalls interspersed throughout sets of strong rapids. At the southern end of the Falls Chain sits stunning Silver Falls. Here, paddlers must complete a 130-rod portage around the water as it passes between Saganaga Lake and the adjacent Saganagons Lake. In canoe country, a rod is approximately the same length as a canoe, 16.5 feet.

The morning of June 1 arrived with more wind, rain, and otherwise unpleasant weather. Now wearing sweatshirts, hats, rain gear, and whatever else they could find in order to stay warm, the six paddlers broke down their camp in relative silence and prepared for a long day of travel. The idea was to make it through the Falls Chain, then paddle Cache Bay and the section of Sag from the bay's mouth back to American Point. They would camp there for the night. Guides from Tuscarora were scheduled to pick them up the following day.

Breaking camp in the wind and rain is not ideal on a camping trip. The half-dozen canoe campers did their required tasks reluctantly and loaded all their gear into the canoes. It was a short paddle to the first portage and all six declined to wear their life jackets. Several opted to clip their life jackets to the seats of each canoe during the portage, as it was one less thing to have to carry. Wearing a life jacket on a portage trail is an option, but they become bulky and burdensome if you're also carrying a pack or portaging a canoe. In addition, the group had not been wearing their life jackets for most of the trip thus far, and habits can be hard to break on the tail end of a canoe trip—even if advisable.

For many weary hours, the group tromped through the Falls Chain. Finally, by early afternoon, they reached Silver Falls and their final portage of the trip. Protected by the dense forest and narrow waterway of the chain, it was likely difficult to tell how windy and intense the weather had become throughout the morning and early afternoon. Progress toward American Point was the only goal. Nobody spoke much as they slogged on.

After completing the 130-rod portage around Silver Falls, the anxious crew soon paddled past another group camped in the far northwest arm of Cache Bay. The other party said they were holding tight for the day as the conditions were not safe for their level of proficiency. Indeed, large white-capped waves were steadily rolling across the main body of Sag and Cache Bay.

At 3:30 p.m., the three canoes and six paddlers were slowly navigating southeast through Cache Bay. Relentless wind and driving rain made for slow progress. Their paddling lacked any type of rhythm as the rolling waves continually disrupted their momentum. Nonetheless, the group managed to move along in a way that did not seem excessively dangerous to the adventurers.

"We were young guys and full of confidence," Hargis said. "We felt invincible for most of that trip."

Within eyesight of the ranger station where Matichuk was busy finishing her daily tasks, the weary paddlers forged ahead. Whitecaps continued to decorate the tops of the relentless waves. Finally sensing the danger of the situation, Mark stopped paddling for a brief moment to put on his life jacket. Rob, who was in the stern, did the same. Mimicking their behavior, Peter and Jeff, who were sharing another canoe, put on their personal floatation devices. Scott and Tom did not follow suit.

"I don't know why they didn't put their life jackets on in that moment," Mark said. "It was a dicey situation and we were just trying to keep moving forward."

Moments later, as the group exited the mouth of Cache Bay and pushed out into the open channel that leads to the heart of Sag, disaster struck. Peter and Jeff's canoe was the first to capsize. The two men entered the churning water and immediately lost all sense of direction. Their life jackets, firmly attached to their bodies, kept them afloat as they gasped for air.

Peter and Jeff had become somewhat separated from the group leading up to their canoe capsizing. The other four paddlers did not see the craft turn over, but soon realized what had occurred. Both canoes turned back toward their friends to help them get to shore. Wind made communication difficult and the waves added to the fray. Despite a challenging sequence, both canoes reached their floating friends and instructed them to continue swimming toward a nearby island.

Seconds later, the next canoe turned over. This time, it was Scott and Tom who entered the lake. The young men were immediately zapped by the cold water. It felt as though electricity was pulsing through their veins. Amid the chaos, Scott was able to don his life jacket after he found it floating near him in the water. Tom tried to do the same. He had mounted the overturned canoe, but in his first attempt to secure the life preserver, he slid off and into a free float on the roiling waters of Sag. This newfound and unwanted freedom was terrifying. Ackerman lunged back toward the canoe. The life jacket, tied up in the waves, pulled away. He let go of the canoe again, kicking and swimming with every ounce of strength he could find, trying to recover the jacket, but it was gone. Tom returned to the canoe once more.

Bearing witness to this perilous scene, Mark and Rob screamed at the four men in the water, instructing them to swim toward a small landmass near the shoreline on the U.S. side of Sag called Spam Island. Spam Island is about the size of a small cabin and features a collection of spruce trees and several skinny, albeit tall red pines. The island gave the four desperate men a chance—something to swim toward. Tom, the only one not wearing a life jacket at this point, was struggling to stay afloat.

After Mark and Rob established that the four swimmers had a plan, they set their sights on paddling back to Matichuk and the Cache Bay Ranger

Station. They were now between Alcorn Island and Spam Island, somewhere in the vicinity of the invisible international border line. Turning back to the north, they pulled fast and hard with their paddles. They reached the mouth of Cache Bay, where the waves change direction in an instant. A funnel directed the wind around Cache Point and into the bay toward the ranger station. Waves four feet high rolled in from behind their canoe. Three consecutive swells poured over and into their defenseless watercraft. As though being pulled by an merciless force looming at the bottom of Sag, the canoe started to sink.

"All that stuff about your life flashing before your eyes is true," Mark said. "Right then, my life flashed before my eyes."

All six men were now in the water. Scott, Tom, Peter, and Jeff were swimming toward Spam Island. Meanwhile, Mark and Rob started their journey toward Alcorn Island, which was not far from where their canoe went down. Though the last to enter the water, Mark and Rob were the first to reach land. Once they did, Mark scrambled upon the rocks, screaming a bloodcurdling plea in desperation. It was incoherent yelling, though he did manage to say "help" several dozen times over the course of a minute. Steep banks on the island added to the chaos and difficulty, at one point causing Mark to tumble backward to the water's edge. The fall wrenched his neck, but when he stood, he continued to scream.

This was the sound Janice heard. It was his

series of desperate wails that sent her into action.

Within seconds of Mark's piercing screams, Tom went below the surface for the first time. Scott, fighting his own struggle for survival, could only watch. Without a life jacket on, Tom simply could not stay afloat any longer. After disappearing for approximately three seconds, he reemerged and gasped for air. He dog-paddled a few more lethargic strokes, gazing blankly at the waves crashing upon him, and went down again. Scott continued to swim a side crawl, his own survival dependent on his careful conservation of energy. Following several large bubbles at the surface, Tom came up once again for air. This time, he did not attempt to swim further toward Spam Island. He did not utter any words. The young man with dreams of graduate school and a good life gently inhaled, then went down again. There was nearly 150 feet of water from the surface where Tom took his last breath to the lakebed. He would die before he reached the bottom.

Yelling at the top of his lungs, Mark could now hear Janice as she roared away from the Cache Bay Ranger Station toward the trouble that drew her. She saw Mark and Rob waving their arms frantically in the air, and veered for Alcorn Island. When she neared where they stood, she could barely make out through their wild gestures and incoherent pleas that their friends were in trouble on the far shore near Spam Island. Once she had confirmed that the two men were safe on Alcorn, she opened up the engine to full throttle and crashed across the international border line. She saw two canoes floating upside down as she neared Spam Island. When the waves broke just right, she could also see gear floating, scattered in the water. Then she saw someone slowly stagger from the water's edge onto shore. It was Scott Black. Janice maneuvered her boat up to the half-frozen man and helped him gingerly climb aboard.

Also on Spam Island and lost in the frenzy of their own desperation, were Peter and Jeff. They were attempting to start a fire, a notion the ranger quickly dismissed when she pulled her boat to shore.

"Is there another with you?" she hollered to Scott, who sat shivering in the wind and rain on a metal bench seat in the middle of the small boat.

"He's gone," Black said. "He went down."

Peter and Jeff joined their friend Scott in the boat, and again, Matichuk roared off. She returned to Alcorn Island, where Mark and Rob stood waiting. Mark was overwhelmed to see his friends and family safe in the boat. However, there were only three in addition to the park ranger, who captained from the stern.

"Where's Tom?" Mark asked when he received the boat at the island's rugged shoreline.

"He didn't make it," Scott said.

"What do you mean he didn't make it?"

"He drowned."

The five young men were all on the brink of hypothermia. Matichuk knew this, and she knew her small watercraft was now overloaded and they still had to cross the main body of Cache Bay in order to reach her ranger station. As the final members of the haggard group entered the boat, she eased away and motored forward. This was the same direction Mark and Rob were paddling when their canoe was swamped in the heavy waves. The storm had only intensified throughout her action, and yet, there was no choice. The ranger moved ahead.

With the lake spraying cold water churned by the howling wind, and in a boat overloaded with five young men shivering and huddled to stay alive, crossing Cache Bay that afternoon was a harrowing experience in and of itself. Eventually, they reached the dock of the ranger station. Matichuk hurried the men inside her home, shed their frozen clothes, and wrapped them in heavy blankets. Her son had the fire roaring and now stoked it; soon it neared 80 degrees inside the small cabin. Once the survivors were dry and warm, Matichuk radioed park headquarters to report a possible death. The group of five young men sat in silence.

"It took a while for us to thaw out and to grasp what had happened. Then we sat by the fire and were introduced to her young boy," Peter said nearly twenty years after the incident. "We waited. She was in charge and calmed us down. She saved our lives."

Chapter Two
The Island

On the south-facing wall near the entrance to the Cache Bay Ranger Station, a series of plaques, photographs, and certificates of achievement hang like paintings in a museum. The room where they hang smells like an old wooden cathedral, and indeed, some feel as though they are entering a holy place when they visit the small cabin-like structure straddling the U.S–Canadian border. Among the items stationed on the wall are the Award of Valor, the Governor General Award for providing assistance to others in a selfless manner, the Award of Merit, and the Ministry of Natural Resources Service Award. There are others. Some large in size, some small. All are significant. Though the listed years vary, the name inscribed on each award is the same: Janice Matichuk.

The Award of Valor is among the highest achievements a Canadian citizen can receive, similar to the Presidential Medal of Freedom in the United States. On the back of her Award of Valor, it reads:

"Presented to Janice Matichuk for superlative action and courage in the lifesaving rescue of five canoeists at Quetico Provincial Park on June 1, 2000."

"That one is tough [to look at] sometimes," Matichuk said in a bittersweet tone. She looked solemnly at the unpolished medal.

Twenty years after Ackerman died near the entrance to Cache Bay, his body shutting down before being swallowed by the frigid waters of Saganaga Lake, his friend Mark Hargis still credits two things for why he is alive to share his story: a life jacket and Janice Matichuk.

"Whenever I hear that someone is going to the boundary waters, I let them know they need to wear their life jacket," Hargis said. "Yes, Janice saved me, but only because I gave her a chance to—because I had my life jacket on. Tom didn't have his life jacket on, and this one decision was the difference. If I could go back and change anything in my life, it would be to have Tom put his life jacket on. Without a doubt, it's my biggest regret in life."

Though the awards inside the Cache Bay Ranger Station recognize particular events, in reality, they are a collection of days, months, and years spent on this island for Matichuk. And while she attempted to minimize change to the island and its surrounding landscape, in return, it shaped her in nearly every way.

"Janice *is* Cache Bay," said Matichuk's longtime friend Bonnie Schudy. "It's at the stage now where you can't really imagine one without the other."

The island was the center of Matichuk's

professional life, however, the island was the setting of much more than a job or career for Matichuk. It's where she raised two children. It's where she endured the highs and lows of a marriage. And it's where she met canoeing enthusiasts and outdoor adventurers from across the planet. They are so tied that, in the eyes of many paddlers entering Cache Bay, the ranger station here belongs to Janice. There is little to no separation between her role as park ranger and that of guardian of Cache Bay. Matichuk was the ultimate gatekeeper, according to Schudy. "People come to Cache Bay because they've heard of Janice," she said. "It's so beautiful because she welcomes you, shares her knowledge, and wants to learn about you and from you all at the same time. On top of that, she has this knowledge of Quetico that is unbelievable."

During the past two decades, Schudy has worked at and managed a variety of canoe outfitters along the Gunflint Trail, a winding 56-mile road in northeastern Minnesota that begins in the small Lake Superior community of Grand Marais and then bears northwest. The Gunflint, as locals call the iconic roadway, weaves its way through remote forests and along many dozens of lakes before ending near Saganaga. By most comparisons, Schudy would be considered a rugged individual, having spent many years lugging canoes around, dealing with tourists, and grinding out a career in the North Woods. Most of her time spent working on the Gunflint Trail involves labor many young men would find challenging. She's cleaned canoes, cleared trails of fallen brush, and knows more about snowmobiles than most people ever will. However, Schudy, who speaks with a thick Minnesota accent, admits that her knowledge of the wilderness in the vast canoe country is nothing compared to Matichuk's.

"Janice has this spirit inside of her, this confidence," Schudy said. "It's unmatched. I think it comes from her connection to nature and understanding of how it works out there. Nature has the lead; you follow what it provides or is doing. That's how Janice operates."

Schudy speaks of her Canadian friend with a flattery often reserved for heroes or people one knows only from afar, someone who is a pop-culture icon. And yet, Schudy has literally been in the thick of things with Matichuk, often stomping through brush and sparsely used portage trails just to see what's on the other side. In 2014, Schudy and Matichuk went camping in Quetico without much of an itinerary for their adventure. The idea was to "explore," Matichuk repeatedly told Schudy in the days leading up to their canoe trip.

"We found a campsite that I thought was incredible and would have liked to stay there for a few days," Schudy recalled. "But late in the evening on our first night there, all of a sudden, Janice wants to go paddle to another lake that she'd heard about that was nearby. So we just kind of took off real quick, totally spontaneous. And the next thing you know, we're walking down a portage trail in the dark and there are wolves howling off in the distance and I'm thinking to myself, *What in the world are we doing out here?"*

Ultimately, Schudy said, it worked out for the best. After breaking through the darkness of tree-cover, brilliance shone through from near the portage's end. A stunning lake, even more remote than the last and one that offered a superior camping site, waited for them. The longtime park ranger never once showed any fear, nor did she boast of being an expert. Matichuk, as was often the case in her life, simply went with what felt right in the moment. "Sometimes with Janice, you just have to trust what is happening, what she is doing or leading you into," Schudy said. "She has this certain magic about her. She's not like anyone I have ever known."

Schudy is not alone among my interviewees in making a direct link between Matichuk and the Cache Bay Ranger Station. It's here where she saved lives. Aside from Rob Anderson, Scott Black, and the three members of the Hargis family, there have been dozens more. Men and women from numerous countries. Adolescent and elderly. Families in distress. People on the edge of hypothermia, others suffering from life-or-death lacerations or broken bones. The incidents are too many to remember.

Though she met scores of campers in their best of moments, seeing somebody for the first time while they are in distress put an entirely new spin on her job. "It's an unusual way to meet people, that's for sure," Matichuk said.

Though she was familiar with what goes into the successful rescue of canoeists, Matichuk had known death and failed missions here too. In addition to Tom Ackerman, others have passed away near her island. In August 2019, a Minnesota man died only five miles from her ranger station. He was using the portage trail leading to the Falls Chain when he suffered a fatal heart attack. Aiding in the extraction of Craig Sicard, the 71-year-old portageur, was among the few experiences Janice would take back.

"It was the first time I saw a dead body in all these years in the park. I'd be okay not having to do that again," Matichuk said. Matichuk never did see Ackerman's body. When his body was recovered from Saganaga Lake several days after he drowned near Cache Bay, it took a team of professional recovery divers days of effort and specialized equipment to locate his body in the depths of mighty Sag. Upon extracting his body, Ackerman was almost immediately hidden from view, wrapped up, and transported to a medical examiner.

Death. The most dreaded outcome of any outdoor adventure. Though rare, it is a possible outcome for every permit Matichuk issued, dating back to the mid-1980s. There is the expectation that a ranger would rescue a canoeist in distress if they are able, and if need be, put themselves in peril doing so. Janice fit the mold. Fearless to a fault, yet always with supreme intentionality, Matichuk experienced a primal control of fate during her nearly forty years in Quetico. June 6th, 2020 she would suffer the cruelty of having the tables turned on her.

On a cloudy day in Thunder Bay, a team of medical professionals told the longtime Quetico ranger that she had glioblastoma, an aggressive and ultimately fatal type of brain cancer. With the news, Matichuk knew that her death would most likely be outside the Quetico Park boundaries and away from the island. In any case, the ranger station at Cache Bay and the land surrounding it remains her legacy. Time has secured her place in the history of Quetico. Brain cancer cannot wash away history.

"I'm not getting super introspective about life and death right now," Matichuk said just days after the diagnosis. "I've been that way all my life. At the same time, I'm starting to realize how much it's all meant to me, this island and all these people I've met at Cache Bay over so many years."

I spent several days with Matichuk on the island in September 2018 while she prepared to close down the station at the end of another season in Quetico. Along with my friend and fellow Boundary Waters enthusiast, Matthew Baxley, we listened to Matichuk as she explained the history of her island. We ate thick-cut New York strip steaks cooked medium-rare, sipped on dark roast coffee, and talked of the surrounding waters within the aroma of pine and fresh woodsmoke. Matichuk spoke of history, her own and that of the island, in a way that had Baxley and me sitting wide-eyed like children. It was as though her stories came from another world, though we sat in the immediate surroundings where many of the stories took place. Not knowing at the time that we were sharing her space in one of her final years on the island, most of our questions focused on her early years in Quetico.

Matichuk was 30 years old when she first arrived at Cache Bay. It was May 1985, and at the time, she was married to a man named Peter Puddicombe. Years later, they would divorce, a topic Matichuk was not often open to discussing publicly.

"There's a lot of pain there," Matichuk told me one afternoon about her splintered marriage, more than a year after I visited the island with Baxley.

At the time of their arrival to Cache Bay in 1985, the couple had just finished building a log cabin on the shores of Tilden Lake, a remote setting near North Bay, Ontario, four hours north of Toronto. The property was some 800 miles from Quetico, so the new location didn't make much sense on paper—at least no paper with a map upon it.

Both Peter and Janice were employed by the Ministry of Natural Resources (MNR) in the spring of 1985, with their assignment focused primarily on promoting canoeing and outdoor recreation near Marten River Provincial Park and the forests surrounding North Bay. They also sold firewood to supplement their income, and the plan was to set up shop in this part of Ontario for the long haul.

And then a fateful letter arrived.

Matichuk's friend, Sally Burns, drafted the letter in late April 1985, suggesting that her longtime friend, Janice, apply for an opening in Quetico. The job that Burns—a spirited outdoorswoman who began working in Quetico in the 1970s—noted in her message was for an interior ranger position at Cache Bay, located on Saganaga Lake, just north of the Minnesota-Ontario border. Having been raised on the north side of the park in the small community of Atikokan, Matichuk was no stranger to the remote wilderness setting and park operations. Both of Matichuk's parents did various contract work inside the park during the 1960s and 70s when Janice was a child.

Despite this familiarity with the park as a whole, the southern portion straddling the U.S. border was largely a mystery to Matichuk. "We always came in from the north and stayed in that part of the park," she said.

The letter from Burns arrived on a Friday. That weekend, Janice called on the input of a few friends and family in and around Atikokan. Monday morning, she put her name into the candidate pool, and by Tuesday, she had the job.

Dave Elder was the superintendent of Quetico from 1973 to 1987. A conversation between him and Cal Osborne, Matichuk's supervisor at the MNR post near North Bay, made the decision to hire Matichuk an easy one. Elder had called Osborne for a reference and to learn about her work ethic, and Osborne kept it simple. "I'll be sorry to lose her." That was good enough recommendation from one seasoned manager to another.

When Elder called Matichuk to inform her that

she'd been selected as the ranger at Cache Bay, her reaction was a mixed bag of excitement and uncertainty.

"I told Dave I didn't know what to pack," Janice said. "I didn't even know what the island looked like. I had no idea."

Elder told Janice not to worry about the specifics. "Show up," he instructed, "learn as you go, apply your knowledge of the wilderness, and greet visitors to the park."

"I knew I could handle the job, the people, and paddlers," Matichuk said. "That didn't worry me. I just didn't know what we'd eat, where we would sleep, how big the whole place was, that sort of thing."

Putting her unease into productivity, Matichuk acquired and began freezing four months' worth of meat to be stored in the island's small propane-powered freezer. It was mostly ground beef, though chicken and sausages were on the list as well. As most things went for Matichuk, everything was rationed, scheduled, budgeted, and considered.

"I even figured out how many times I was going to have my period while there and brought enough tampons," she told me in 2019, with matter-of-fact practicality in her voice.

I did not know how to respond. It made sense, but her frankness sometimes caught my tongue.

Joining Peter and Janice on the island that first year was their five-month-old daughter, Ingela, and their dog, Strangelove. They arrived with more than 2,000 lbs. of gear, including a crib, dog food, and canned goods. A plane brought rations twice a month to provide fresh produce and other items with a short shelf life. The resupplies were helpful, but in truth, they were small comfort to their dramatic change in lifestyle. Once they arrived in the spring of 1985, the family didn't leave the park interior for the entirety of their first summer in residence. By taking the job, they in fact couldn't leave—it being a requirement that the on-site ranger be at or near the ranger station 24 hours a day, seven days a week, for the entire season.

"We never had a day off, and that's the way we liked it," Matichuk said.

Operations at Cache Bay fell into a routine rather quickly for Janice, Peter, and Ingela during their first year on the island. Issuing permits, then completed with pen and paper, was a key task. As was behind-the-scenes work, including firewood production, maintenance on the cabin, reporting weather conditions, and answering questions about anything from hot fishing spots, scenic canoe routes, to Shangri-La campsites. There was admittedly a lot of improvised work completed during those first years, but it was obvious that Matichuk was a natural fit for the position.

"I fell in love with the island right away," she said. "The first walk from the dock up to the cabin, I knew without a doubt that this is where I am meant to be. Once we got here, I never stopped to consider if it was the right move. It was, and it still is a lot of hard work. But I've loved it from the beginning."

Despite having to become more familiar with

the many miles of portage trails, lake names, and faces—those familiar and not—of the paddling community who cherished Quetico, the one thing Matichuk came prepared for on day one was hard work. To describe Matichuk's work ethic as intense or unyielding would be like judging the pink and gold energy of a summer sunrise over Lake Superior to be merely *okay* or *decent*—a gross understatement to say the least.

Matichuk constantly made herself busy, preferably physical labor that involved using her hands. A never-ending chore list spun through her mind the way people get songs stuck in their head. Some, principally Matichuk herself, consider that restlessness a form of worldly discontent. The other side of that coin is the power and usefulness of simple motivation. Hard work was in her blood. Sometimes, her motivation was relentless to a fault. Despite a surgically repaired rotator cuff, she still insisted on splitting wood with an axe into her last season.

So, naturally, on most of my visits to her island, she insisted on doing chores while we talked. She then would stack split wood with speed and precision, the way an experienced chess player sees the totality of plays from start to finish before the first move.

"You have to think about where the last piece is going to fit on the pile, not just the first," Matichuk explained in her typical fashion, transforming a normally mundane task into one as complex as spinal surgery.

This lifestyle wasn't easy on her body, much

beyond the periodic shoulder pain. Standing at just over 5'4" tall, Matichuk said she started her tenure at Cache Bay about an inch and a half taller.

"Carrying firewood, rocks, and boxes of supplies from the dock to the cabin has squashed me down," she said with a modest laugh.

Aside from a possible reduction in height, Matichuk had physically changed surprisingly little over the years. Photos from when she started on the island show her hair was a dishwater blonde, short, and often curly. Later, it hung long with a subtle mixture of brown and gray. Her arms were accustomed to hard work, demonstrated by her sinewy muscles at work, her hands taut and weathered, evidenced whenever she checked things off from her perpetual to-do list.

And though she had this lean toughness to her, it did not define her. Instead, friends and colleagues speak first of her kindness. Among those who do is Tom McCann, a northeastern Minnesota resident and longtime paddler of the Boundary Waters region. An accomplished artist and one-time gardener for famed wilderness author Sigurd Olson, McCann said Matichuk was an ambassador for Quetico and the paddling community.

"She represents the legacy of managers and rangers of the park," he said. "And she represents the values shared by the people of Ontario. It's her work ethic. It's her knowledge of the land, the weather there, and her island."

Even at the time of our interviews, Matichuk

was still more tough and more able than most men, and certainly men her age. She was born July 24, 1954, in Atikokan, which sits about 2½ hours west of the Lake Superior port-town Thunder Bay. She had blue eyes that told her story whether she wanted them to or not. Like her voice, her eyes colored the memories of adventure, pain, grief, curiosity, and creativity whenever she shared.

She was very proud to be both Canadian and Ontarian, and by happenstance, her favorite colors since childhood had been blue and green, something that had always drawn her amusement.

"It turns out now those are the Ontario Park logo colors," she said with a genuine laugh. "Synchronicity!"

Atikokan, the headquarters of the six primary ranger stations throughout Quetico, is lovingly dubbed "The Canoeing Capital of Canada." The other ranger stations are found around the perimeter of the park and include Dawson Trail, Beaverhouse Lake, Lac La Croix, Prairie Portage, and Cache Bay. Matichuk spent many spring, summer, and fall evenings during her first years in Quetico exploring the landscape around Cache Bay. The routine work schedule of the park service kept her focused on duties and assignments around the station for most of the day. Whenever she had time, though, Matichuk was quick to explore. She plodded the assorted portages, paddled the lakes, streams, and bogs, and checked up on campsites in a tireless quest to know her domain inside and out. On her days off, while

Peter covered the ranger station, she would sometimes roam beyond the bay, traveling more than 25 miles in a single day just to get a feel for what stood at the other side of the next portage.

"I wanted to be able to tell people who came through Cache Bay what it's like out there," Matichuk said. "And I wanted to see it with my own eyes, not just by looking at the map or in the guidebook."

The structure that now serves as the Cache Bay Ranger Station was built in 1957. Up until then, the ranger station had been located on a peninsula known as Cache Point. That small cabin was built in 1933. After two decades of operating the ranger station from the point, park officials determined it was too difficult for resupply planes to access and selected the nearby island as its replacement. The facilities that served the original Cache Bay Ranger Station were modest structures by all accounts, with one of the original cabins no larger than "the front porch of the current cabin," Matichuk pointed out.

Modest in its own right, the station at Cache Bay still looks essentially the same as it did when eager canoeists paddled up seeking Matichuk's guidance that first year working in Quetico. All of the buildings, including the cabin that serves from May until September as both ranger station and Matichuk's home, are located on the south side of the island. There is also a small bunkhouse, a composting latrine facility that looks as if it's been plucked from a rest stop, a boathouse-storage building, a communication tower, and several solar panels to power some of the operations.

As paddlers approach from the main body of Sag and bear north into Cache Bay, they pull up to a floating dock that extends from the southeastern tip of the island. Enormous red and white pines stand proudly near the ranger station and are spread across the small expanse. A teal sign reading Quetico Cache Bay marks the location. A meter that indicates the day's fire danger for Quetico stands nearby, impossible to miss. Above the meter fly two large flags: one, the Canadian colors, the other, Ontario's provincial flag. After securing one's canoe to the dock, visitors are greeted by the island's slightly inclined face, welcoming them to the main entrance of the ranger station. There, Matichuk was ready to issue permits and offer advice on routes, safety, and what to expect paddling Quetico.

For decades, this had been the routine. Paddlers showed up, and Matichuk completed the required paperwork while doing her best to inform the group or individual how best to take in Quetico.

It could be that cut and dried. Canoes come; canoes go. Matichuk, though, was not wired this way. After the formalities were finished, it was time to get to know the guests. Far from making pleasantries, Matichuk was genuinely curious about each group. Everyone came from somewhere different, for different reasons, with different expectations. Over the course of more than 30 years, Matichuk's life was intertwined with the thousands who passed through the wilderness that she called home.

Francis Walsh, a Rochester, Minnesota native, first met Matichuk in 1989 when he was a teenager.

"That was my first trip to Quetico," Walsh recalled. "As often happens, that trip pretty much sealed my fate—Quetico was my home, and Cache Bay would forever be the center of that home."

In my conversations with him, Walsh referred to Matichuk as the "guardian angel of Quetico's entire east side," and because of her gravity, Walsh preferred to camp in or near Cache Bay on his Quetico trips. It was common for Matichuk to paddle out in the early evenings, after her day's work was complete, for a conversation with her friend.

"She often stops and visits around my campfire, or right near the water's edge and just catches up." Walsh offered his preference, though. "I paddle out and then hole up on a little outcropping I call 'the talking point,'" he recalled.

Not all of Matichuk's stories involve harrowing rescues or are full of grand adventure. In fact, most aren't. A common Janice campfire tale that Walsh and other paddlers would hear is from 2008 when Matichuk arrived to open the ranger station for the season.

"That was the year my cabin was vandalized," Matichuk said, pausing to time the punch line's delivery. "Yep, first time it was ever broken into."

As the curious listener waits to hear more, Matichuk builds tension before explaining that it was a pine marten, not a person, responsible for the vandalism.

"The rotten critter ate all of my dehydrated camping food—and that's expensive stuff!" the story goes. "Then it must have had diarrhea from the volume of dried food because the room stunk, which I initially thought was going to be from some decomposed animal, but nope, it was stink from excrement."

Of course, most of Matichuk's stories come from Cache Bay, a secluded world where some of the steep granite cliffs are honored with pictographs from the Indigenous community, who have lived in the border lakes region for generations.

Though in many ways distinct, Cache Bay is an extension of the much larger body of Saganaga Lake. The bay is prone to severe weather, waves, and natural intensity like that of the heart of the lake, says Becky Kayser, a friend of Matichuk who owns a cabin with her husband, Dick, on the eastern side of Canadian Sag.

"Janice is ideal to live at the ranger station at Cache Bay because she lives and breathes the lifestyle," Kayser says. It is not hyperbole to say that Janice's life and the life of the park were one. "Janice is devoted, strong, and caring. She has been a consistent professional devoted to the ideals of Quetico."

Trevor Gibb became the superintendent of Quetico Provincial Park in March 2014. At the time, he was in his early 30s and already had an abundance of experience working in provincial parks across Ontario, notably as the assistant superintendent at

Polar Bear Provincial Park.

This remote outpost, the largest of Ontario's parks, is located where James and Hudson Bays meet and can only be accessed by plane—so remote that Quetico is a relative metropolis. It is also a safeguard for the world's southernmost population of polar bears. And the toughest being in all of his encounters?

"Nothing fazes Janice," Gibb says. "She's dedicated, diligent, strong, professional, and resourceful. She's a problem-solver." No matter where he has worked or traveled in the Ontario parks system, or for that matter, anywhere outside it, he says he has never come across someone quite like Janice Matichuk.

Park officials, including Gibb, are not shy about the impact Matichuk has had on the Cache Bay Ranger Station. It's common to hear paddlers and officials refer to the station as "Janice's Island." Though most of the island remains undisturbed by humans, it is very clear when visiting the ranger station that Matichuk helped shape the identity of the natural wonder.

"Her love for the station and the island can be seen in her charming added touches all around the station," Gibb says.

These unique touches Gibb describes include more than three decades of Matichuk's personality spilling out across the island. Small stones stacked on each other in seemingly impossible ways, homemade and artistic signs secured here and there informing guests where to locate the latrine, where to pick up permits, and the like. Natural treasures from around the park are also displayed for the public eye, including moose sheds and pinecones the size of footballs. Inside her personal half of the cabin, Matichuk's shelves were filled with artwork, stones, and collected memories. A shelf above the wood stove contained everything from birch bark art to tiny shells from centuries past.

"I like to see who notices what," Matichuk said of her tiny treasures. "It tells you a lot about people, what they notice or pick up on."

Throughout my conversation with Walsh, he hammers home Matichuk's deep connection to the natural world. "She sees beauty in things that most of us would walk by without so much as a glance," he tells me. "Janice has packed away so many rocks and bones and skulls and sticks and eggshells and feathers from Cache Bay over the years that they fill her island cabin. Each artifact is loved and cherished, sometimes to tears."

Maybe most important of all, as the assigned guardian of this threshold, Matichuk knew full well that Cache Bay is the entrance to paradise for many; she understood and appreciated its beauty firsthand. Each tree has meaning here. Each storm, each season. Each paddler, each experience. Matichuk knew and appreciated that each canoe trip here is a grand experience for those involved. They are here to experience something the world beyond Quetico cannot offer them. Those paddling through for the first time are eager to experience what others have only told them about, or simply what their minds have imagined. As canoe campers arrived to the ranger station while we talked and worked, it was quickly evident that Matichuk was fully aware and appreciative of the power and natural wonder she looked over each day, each year.

"Janice breathes the air from Cache Bay more deeply than anyone I know," Walsh says. "She holds each breath to the point of nearly passing out. I love her for it."

Chapter Three
A Place in the Pines

Janice Matichuk's first job was devoted to keeping people safe. She was in the fifth grade at the time, or as Canadians refer to it, grade five. For this highly esteemed position, it was her responsibility to help other children navigate oncoming traffic—she was a crossing guard. Naturally, she worked very hard and took the job very seriously.

"I couldn't believe it when the principal asked me to take it on," Matichuk said, more than 50 years later. "I felt like I was this nobody in the back of the class, and suddenly, I had this huge responsibility."

Matichuk admitted the crossing guard duties were quite basic and universal—even if they didn't feel that way at the time. She *had* to make sure her classmates maneuvered the streets and sidewalks safely when school was done for the day. In her mind, the job was paramount to nearly everything else happening in her own little universe.

"Looking back, I can see that when I was asked to do this is when everything changed for me," Matichuk said. "It seems like such a silly moment in the grand scheme of things, but that's when it became

47

clear that I just wasn't wired the same as everyone else."

Matichuk said she often stayed up at night replaying various situations where things could have gone wrong in her role as a crossing guard. She needed to work harder and be prepared for anything, she would obsessively tell herself. She knew she was always capable of doing better.

"I took it way too seriously," she said. "I was stupidly responsible, and that practice carried over into so many things. It still does in some ways."

Matichuk attended grade school and grew up in Atikokan. It's not a bustling tourist destination in terms of charm and charisma, though many do consider it a nice place to live. Established in 1899, the community's roots are industrial. Historically, mining and forestry have paid the majority of mortgages and car loans for the town's residents, though for many, those incomes are now in the rear-view mirror.

Aged buildings line the main street through town. Full-size pickups, locally referred to as "half-tons," are common in most residential driveways. Chevy Silverados. Ford F-150s. Dodge Rams. They're all there.

The Atikokan River meanders its way through town, lined by streets wide enough for logging trucks that haul timber from the nearby forests. The trendy marketing efforts that have helped towns of similar size in the boundary waters region attract tourists and diversify their economies—notably Grand Marais,

Minnesota—are grandiose in comparison to the relative ambition in Atikokan. It is a simple Ontario town where canoeing, snowmobiling, hard work, forestry, and family are the focus of most people's lives. It's the way people who live here want it to be, according to Matichuk.

"The town has gotten smaller since I was a kid growing up here in the 60s," Matichuk told me on a crisp autumn afternoon in the waning days of the ranger station's operational season. The sun shone through the island's red pines onto a calm Sag, setting progressively earlier as the days grew shorter. The scene felt like a metaphor of Atikokan's last sixty years. "There were more than 7,000 people living here back then. Now, there's about 2,000. Other than that, it's got the same feel. The same look."

Matichuk still owned a home in her hometown and typically lived there when the Cache Bay Ranger Station was closed for winter.

Her three-and-a-half decade routine changed in 2020. The change was initially temporary—because of the COVID-19 pandemic, the border and the Cache Bay entrance to Quetico remained closed to start the 2020 paddling season. Matichuk was further destined for a summer at home after being diagnosed with terminal brain cancer. These impediments sadly kept her from working her entire last season. 2020 was the first summer Matichuk spent at home in 35 years.

"It feels really strange being here," she said in a June 2020 phone conversation. "I'm not seeing the campers I see every year. I'm not doing all the chores that require physical labor. It's a whole new thing being here in Atikokan during the summer when I am so used to being on the island."

Matichuk and her two younger brothers, Craig and Darcy, were all born in Atikokan and to this day, her family remains strongly tied to northwestern Ontario. Both of her now-adult children remain in the area. Darcy still lives in Atikokan, working as an electrician; Craig, who worked as a millwright for most of his adult life, passed away in 1999.

Janice's parents, Sam and Anne, settled in Atikokan after Sam found work dredging a nearby lake so that it could be mined for iron ore. At the time, Atikokan had one of the highest birth rates in all of Canada, and the boom-bust cycle common for most mine towns was in full swing. Around the same time, Minnesota's Iron Range was reaching its mid-century peak. Extraction was a mainstay of industry and jobs doing so were plentiful on both sides of the border.

Sam Matichuk met his would-be wife in the remote town of Kashabowie, about an hour drive east of Atikokan. He was living as if straight out of a Woody Guthrie song, working for the railroad industry and living in the woods.

"We lived on the outskirts of our little town and we were always exploring the lakes and everything around us," Sam told me. "We were always camping and getting outdoors doing one thing or another."

Talking with Sam Matichuk about his daughter was a fascinating experience. He got directly to examining her many accomplishments and accolades collected from her time at Cache Bay over the years. He chose his words most carefully as he described her work ethic. The elder Matichuk settled in while explaining in his low, deep voice, "Janice always wanted to get out there and work hard, give it everything she had." It's obvious that Sam was proud of the life his daughter led, and in particular, how who she was helped make her career at Cache Bay. Sam brought almost every question about his daughter back to her natural passion and enthusiasm for the woods and waters of Ontario, his respect for Janice revealing itself as our conversion unfolded. "She was always out there running around in the woods, always past supper and everything. She just liked it, even from a very young age," he said.

Long before he reached retirement, Sam's hands were worn raw from decades of hard labor. Now long retired, though still very much practiced, Sam carved out a living as an electrician, plumber, and general handyman and laborer over the course of his life. Some of that labor included occasional visits to Cache Bay and work in the wider Quetico wilderness.

"I went to all of those ranger stations over the years," Sam said. "I would make it a point to ask the rangers what they felt the setups and cabins needed to be improved or upgraded. They were the ones living and working there. They would know more than someone at a desk somewhere else."

The Matichuk family lived a simple life while Janice and her brothers were growing up. There was always enough food on the table, but any form of *vacation* simply meant camping in the nearby forests. Janice said herself, "The family slept in the bush for our vacations, maybe out on an island on a lake somewhere not necessarily far from town."

In Canada, *the bush* is often used in place of the word *wilderness*. It refers to areas where the timber stands are thick and pavement is lacking or altogether absent. Around here, red pines hundreds of years old stand guard. It's where the water is cold and pure. It was here that Janice had always been most at home. "She was always out there walking in the forests, looking at moss on the rocks, staring up into the trees way up there," her father said, briefly looking up, a proud smile upon his face.

During my stay at the Cache Bay Ranger Station as the 2018 season waned, Matichuk told stories about her favorite red pines on the island as though she was sharing stories of old friends. Large and living seasonal acquaintances, Matichuk missed certain trees during the winter, she explained. Indeed, Matichuk was not shy when it came to sharing the fact that she talked out loud to the trees while nobody else was around. This appeared to hold true even when others *were* around, as became evident in the three days that my friend Matthew Baxley and I spent on the island that September.

"I tell them I love them," she said, gesturing to a pair of towering red pines standing not far from the ranger station. "I hug them in the spring when I get back here. I ask them what they saw over the winter. I tell them how I am doing. We're friends. Call me crazy if you want to. These trees are my friends. It's in my DNA, this connection to the trees and rocks and everything out here."

The Matichuk name comes from the Ukraine, where Sam's father carried it from in the early 1900s, across the Atlantic on his way to Canada and a new life. Janice's grandfather, Sam Sr., arrived first on the Eastern seaboard of North America, but his journey soon continued. He headed north and west across the frozen tundra of subarctic Canada, and along the way, met another Ukrainian immigrant named Anne Repay. Anne was living in the far north already, her family settling in the Northwest Territories, directly east of Alaska and the Yukon. This was, and remains a harsh and diverse landscape, even by Canadian standards. It is home to significant populations of grizzly and polar bears. The rare wood bison still stomps through the mosquito-laden bogs and streams of this spongy terrain. Perhaps seeking a more pleasant path forward in their new country, Sam Sr. and Anne married quickly before settling in a remote area of Saskatchewan to raise a family.

Janice and her two younger brothers did not form much of a relationship with their father's side of the family for geographical reasons. Travel was difficult when there was only so much money to spend, and the great distances that separate communities in rural Canada made it a challenge to stay in contact with certain people, even family, given the lack of technological connection at the time. This is a reality many Canadians that grew up in the early to middle part of the 20th century knew all too well, the Matichuks no different.

Janice was, however, able to form a deep relationship with her maternal grandmother, Betty. Soon after arriving on a ship from Sweden in 1923, Betty met her future husband, another Swedish immigrant named Olie Carlson. Thousands of Swedish immigrants arrived to Canada and a number of American states, including Minnesota, during this time period. The boreal forests of central Canada and the boundary waters in particular are similar to the terrain found in many parts of Scandinavia. In a lot of ways, the familiar land made the adjustment for the immigrants who arrived from Northern Europe, including Matichuk's grandparents, easier.

Betty and Olie met in Winnipeg but eventually moved to the mining community of Elliot Lake, Ontario, just north of Lake Huron. Olie found steady work there at the Stanrock Mine, a notorious uranium mine. As it turns out, the job ultimately cost him his life, at least according to Janice. After a long and dedicated career working in the mine, Olie died in his early 50s from silicosis, a disease that comes from breathing hazardous dust for extended periods of time.

Janice was 11 years old when her grandpa Olie passed. She'd just started her duties as a crossing guard and the world was seemingly growing more complex by the day. As if the seriousness of the crossing guard duties weren't enough pressure on little Janice, she now had death to ponder as well. Matichuk told me it was around this time that she began to reflect on life and what happens when someone dies. She said it never created a sense of fear or dread, but rather a circular feeling. As we discussed these essential parts of life, she expressed feeling past lives and future lives, a natural balance.

After Olie died, Janice's grandmother Betty was not up for living alone so far away from her family, so she filled a massive trunk with her possessions and moved west to live in Atikokan. "Grandma Betty was a very simple woman, but she was highly motivated," Janice said.

Betty rented a small building on Main Street and quickly got to work. The front of the building served as a store where she sold fabric remnants. The back was her house. Out of a tiny backroom, Betty slept, cooked, and lived.

"She had a single bed and dresser," Janice recalled. "She cooked all of her meals on a hot plate and washed her dishes in the bathroom sink."

Despite the seeming hardship, Betty remained herself, unencumbered by the new way of life. One afternoon, Betty stopped by the Matichuk household for what appeared to be a casual visit. To everyone's surprise, she walked in the front door holding an accordion. She'd acquired the instrument years before, but it hadn't had any attention since the move to Atikokan. When Betty arrived that afternoon with the instrument in hand, she was ready to play. Loudly.

"She just murdered that thing," Janice said of her grandmother's ability to play the accordion. To some, even good accordion playing is challenging on the ears. Bad accordion playing takes that pain to a whole new level. Janice reasoned the easiest way to get the instrument out of Betty's hands was to play it herself, an elegant solution. There and then, at age 12, Janice began playing the accordion. To this day, it's her favorite instrument.

"I was never very good at it, but I love the sound it makes," Janice said. "When I was young, they would put me in a chair and literally tie the accordion to me, then tie me to the chair so I wouldn't fall off and could see over the top of the thing."

Perhaps in the interest of everyone in the household, Betty paid for Janice to be taught how to play. The gesture was modest, but it meant a great deal to Janice. "I knew she didn't have any money," Janice said. "For her to do something like that because she knew I liked the sound it made, that was something I never forgot."

Meanwhile, Janice said the accordion did little to improve her social stature among peers. She describes feeling during this time of her life as "the kid who lived on the other side of the tracks." In a small community, living even a few miles outside of town had an impact on the social dynamics for her.

"I wasn't outgoing. I had this accordion, which wasn't a popular instrument when all these rock bands were on the scene. I was just out there on my own," she said.

She did have something that nobody could take away from her, though, her love of the natural world. The water. The trees. The earth. The wildlife. Nature made sense to young Janice's eyes, hands, and spirit. She would spend hours, day after day, wandering through the forest. It was not hunting or even foraging that appealed to her. It wasn't even entertainment or thrills she sought. More than anything, the nearby woods "just felt like home." It was around this time that Matichuk first started to talk out loud to the forest, especially to the oldest trees she could find.

"I never really got much into being popular in school, growing up," Matichuk told me one morning over coffee. "It wasn't something that mattered to me. I found out later that some of the boys had a big crush on me or whatever. But I just wasn't concerned about the social thing or staying out late or getting into trouble. It just wasn't me."

As the years went by, Matichuk recognized that she wanted to have a career that was outdoors. It was essential that she be on her feet and connected to the natural world. With this in mind, Matichuk was accepted into the forestry technician program at Sault College in Sault Ste. Marie, Ontario. The year was 1972 and she was among the first women to enroll in this program at the university.

"It's what I wanted to do," Matichuk said. "I didn't care about the man or woman thing. Can I do this or not was the real question. I knew I could. So I applied and got in."

In 2020, a quick glance at the Sault College

forestry technician page of the school's website shows two young women in the forest taking field samples and measurements from a stand of trees. The women sport hardhats and reflective safety vests. Both of the students appear to be genuinely interested in the work they're doing. On one hand, it's safe to assume that the college is showcasing that not all of the learning in this education program takes place stuck at a desk in a classroom. On the other, it's an obvious pitch that the path for women to make a career in forestry is there should they choose to walk it. This is the same path upon which Matichuk helped lay the foundation decades ago.

"That wasn't on my mind at the time and it never really was while I was in school," Matichuk said. "I was comfortable doing the work and being outside. It was not about trying to break barriers or something like that. I never thought of myself as a pioneer in anything until people pointed it out to me later and then I thought about it some, or saw what they meant. But I never set out to do anything like that or did it just for that reason."

Despite her choice to major in a traditionally male-dominated field, college life was kind to Matichuk. She felt accepted by her professors, peers, and classmates, perhaps for the first time in an educational setting. She learned a great deal about forestry, the natural world, and the woods she'd loved since she was a child. Her interests in trees, plants, rocks, and water now had a scientific and historical knowledge to support them. It opened a new path for her natural curiosities to wander.

Even while in college, Matichuk had all kinds of time to roam the nearby forests. Unlike many of her peers, Matichuk didn't pursue the party scene. She was, however, on the college badminton and curling teams. In the classroom and at home she studied hard and her transcript shows she bagged respectable grades. Meanwhile, romanticized notions of life amongst the trees were replaced with technical logging terminology when she spoke about the woods. And while her vocabulary changed, her heart did not.

"It's funny, because I was a tree hugger before that was ever a thing, or at least before people ever really used the term," Matichuk said. "Even when I was learning about the forestry and logging industries, I was still just absolutely in love with trees. So it wasn't just that I was a woman that made me different than most of the people I was around. I looked at the bush differently than most of the people in the forestry school and industry did."

After completing the college program in two years, Matichuk went to Sweden to study forestry in a post-graduate exchange program. The idea was to learn sustainable logging techniques already being practiced throughout Scandinavian countries in the 1970s and bring those back to Ontario. She knew she would have a job waiting for her at the local paper mill and logging company in Ontario when she returned to Canada the following year, as that was all arranged before she left on the overseas trip.

With the opportunity to travel to Sweden came a mixed bag of feelings for Matichuk. On one hand, she would be continuing her education and collecting valuable skills that would boost her marketability as an employee when she returned to Canada. It was also a chance to trace her biological roots in her ancestral homeland. On the other hand, she was leaving Canada for the first time, and with it, all the comforts that made sense to a backwoods northlander who liked to spend Friday nights playing the accordion or whispering to her favorite trees.

"I was excited about going overseas," Matichuk said, "but I was also terrified, I guess you could say. Other than going to forestry school, I had barely been outside of northwestern Ontario."

Matichuk landed in the small community of Hällefors, Sweden, three hours northwest of Stockholm. She had a position lined up with a forestry company on the outskirts of town and moved into a tiny dorm-sized apartment. Two other exchange students lived in the same building, both of whom were also hoping to learn firsthand a variety of forestry practices that differed from what they had read about in college textbooks. Of her co-workers, Matichuk said they were "a guy from Turkey and a guy from Syria. They hated each other and fought like cats and dogs."

The Swedes take their forestry seriously, which is not only evident in practices that focus on replanting and sustainability, but also in the fact that, in 1903, their nation passed the world's first Forestry

Act. Just as Matichuk's grandparents and other immigrants appreciated their chosen section of the new world for its similarity to where they came from, the landscape of central Sweden was not a far stretch of Janice's memory from the wilds of northwestern Ontario. Large stands of timber are interrupted only by the many hundreds of lakes and perhaps the occasional small town. Further increasing her comfort, both women and men had worked in the Swedish timber industry for centuries before her arrival. While Matichuk was viewed by many as a pioneer in the forestry industry in Ontario, in Sweden, she was merely following the boot prints of other women.

Matichuk spent six months living and working in Sweden. Her memories of the experience are fond, though she is more likely to tell a story of her adventures after the conclusion of the work program than she is to discuss Scandinavian sustainable forestry. Indeed, Matichuk traveled across much of Europe after her internship came to a close.

This was a time of intense personal growth for Janice, especially given the difficulty of global communication at the time. For the entirety of her experience overseas, she did not speak on the phone or otherwise verbally communicate with anyone she knew prior to leaving Canada, including her family. She did, however, write letters. Many, many letters.

"I started writing on anything I could find," Matichuk said. "I would write on scrap paper or napkins, anything. I just love to write letters. I love writing and sending letters. It means so much to me."

Seeing the world beyond the boreal forests of northwestern Ontario daily opened Matichuk's eyes to how big and how vast the world truly is. Traveling to the country of some of her forebearers and then across Europe planted various seeds of creativity in her mind. She started to paint and draw colorful images on wood and canvas. Her interest in men and dating and partnership blossomed. A transformation in both the creative and spiritual elements of her psyche unfolded. All the while, she remained focused on what she set out to do: work in and for her familiar forests in the wilds of northwestern Ontario.

It was winter when Matichuk packed her suitcase for the final time in Europe and returned to Canada. Within a matter of days, she was scheduled to start her new job as a forest technician for a company based in Thunder Bay called Great Lakes Forest Products. The company was expanding its logging operations outside the eastern border of Quetico Provincial Park. No logging was allowed within the park, but outside the boundaries, it was very much open for business. Based solely on the brief job description she had found, the gig was ideal for Matichuk.

Amid those frigid winter months, she started performing tree surveys. She was not bothered by the harshness of the elements; this assignment meant she was out of the office, studying the land, and in physical contact with the forest. There was but one drawback in addition to the cold. The forest was full of men.

"I came into these camps and it was rough," Matichuk said. "There were some women who worked as cooks, but all the forestry workers were men." She paused. "It was me. And it was them."

Al Wainwright spent his career working as an engineer for Great Lakes Forest Products, a subsidiary of the Canadian Pacific railroad company, and he was the boss of Janice's boss. While Matichuk strived to be in the forest, Wainwright did most of his work from an office in Thunder Bay, though he would make an effort to get out into the woods whenever possible.

"She was a great worker, I can remember that plain as day," Wainwright told me in Grand Marias one afternoon. "She wanted to be out there and would do whatever needed to be done. Everything with her had to be very thorough when she first started. We had to get that sorted out." He chuckled. "It would just take too long the way she wanted it done to perfection."

At its very core, logging can be an aggressive, primitive industry: see tree; cut tree; take tree. That characteristic of the industry, likewise, has a tendency to draw in characters who are rough around the edges. Because she had a degree in forestry, had studied the trade abroad, and was a highly motivated worker, Matichuk's opinion soon mattered in not one but two separate logging camps. She was not the boss, but she was certainly not at the bottom of the hierarchy. Wainwright readily acknowledged that she climbed the company ladder quickly, and her attitude and work ethic shone a bright spotlight on her future in the logging industry. Meanwhile, testosterone hung heavy in the camps, a dense fog not even her shining light could dispel.

"I had men saying terrible things to me all the time," Matichuk said. "Degrading comments. Sexual innuendos. Awful things."

There were physical encounters too. Sexual advances made by the men in the camps were not unheard of. On rare occasions, rough coworkers with bad teeth and wild eyes would enter her sleeping quarters. Like kicking at a shark in the sea or a grizzly on a mountain trail, sometimes kicking and screaming makes the animal go away, and sometimes it doesn't.

"I was assaulted in the camps, yes, you could say that," Matichuk said, quite matter-of-factly. "It was bloody horrible. I don't know what else I can tell you other than that." It was clear that some memories weren't worth stirring.

Wainwright, who is now long retired and still resides in Thunder Bay, while quick to praise Matichuk and her work ethic all these years later, knew of the darkness she encountered on the job. When it came to Matichuk's life in the logging camps and the crudeness of the men who shared her space, Wainwright did not mince words.

"She was in the depths of hell," he told me.

Matichuk lasted two years in the logging camps. Despite the frigid temperatures that come with logging in the winter and the toxic masculinity that saturated the camps, Matichuk walked away from the gig with full recognition from her superiors that she was a tireless worker who understood the forest in a way most who walk this earth never will.

"She had an appreciation for the natural world," Wainwright said. "We hated to see her go, but we understood."

Wainwright next saw Matichuk as she was riding a motorcycle heading east to Toronto. She told him that she was off to study art and see what the big city had to offer. The artist's spark had found a flame while riding trains across Europe and it needed more fuel. It was once again time to be on the move.

Matichuk made it to Toronto. When she got there, she found more than just bright lights and high rent. On April 1, 1976, she met someone. His name was Peter Puddicombe, her future husband.

After meeting on April Fool's Day, and over the course of the next nine years, Janice and Peter would do everything from competitive canoe racing to carving and selling canoe paddles. Manufacturing paddles from home was merely a side-gig, though, as they eventually picked up steady work for the Ministry of Natural Resources in North Bay. On paper, the couple was a perfect match. All the while, many who knew them, including Janice's father, say the pair were at odds most of the time. Despite the occasional storm, Janice and Peter had their first child, Ingela, not long after they got married. Ingela was six months old when the family arrived at the Cache Bay Ranger Station in the spring of 1985.

Four years later, their second child arrived, this

time, a boy. They named him Leif. Both names, Leif and Ingela, came back with Janice from Sweden. She'd heard the names while traveling abroad and had hoped one day to put them on a birth certificate. And while the names alone might not stand out as entirely unique to somebody with a Swedish bloodline, one fact scribed upon their children's birth certificate certainly does. Ingela and Leif were born exactly four years apart on the same day, at the same hour, and down to the same minute. When asked about this phenomenon, Matichuk kept it simple. "I'm organized." Adept at deadpan as well, I found.

Years later, the family now secure in their roles as the guardians of Cache Bay, Leif's arrival meant the island's population suddenly grew from three to four seasonal residents. Home was still a thousand miles away, on Tilden Lake near North Bay, far beyond Lake Superior and yet further inland across the massive province that is Ontario.

Meanwhile, life on the island for the bustling quartet was just getting started.

Chapter Four
The Bustling Bay

"There are some things you learn best in calm, and some in storm."
—**Willa Cather,** *The Song of the Lark*

It's a strange thing to be charged by a moose. One moment, all is calm. In the next, chaos.

"It's like a freight train with big eyes coming at you." Matichuk said of her encounters with charging moose, holding half-open fists to her face like she was holding a pair of fake binoculars, indicating the unblinking stare of a raging moose.

Due to their enormity, moose are not normally associated with stealth or swiftness. Despite this, when the animal decides to charge, however rare such an event may be, it seems to happen in an instant. Such an occurrence unfolded a number of times during Matichuk's many years working in the Boundary Waters region. Ironically, the most notable and terrifying instances were always when she was in the most similar circumstances to that which notoriously riles wild animals: with children present.

It happened once when Ingela was by her side and twice while Leif was present.

On postcards and photographs, moose are the very definition of wilderness royalty. Majestically strolling across the landscape, appearing no more of a threat than a horse grazing in a fenced pasture. When a moose charges, however, their eyes bulge out of their eye sockets. The animal's ears pin down to the top of their massive skulls. Seemingly every hair on their neck stands on end as though they'd been jolted with electricity. The second time Leif and his mom were charged by a moose, a memorable day in the summer of 1999, he could have quite literally reached out from around the tree he was standing behind and touched the enormous beast as it thundered past.

"I just remember seeing this frothing head go charging by me," said Leif. "I could see the steam coming out of its nostrils."

The incident transpired on the famed Monument Portage, which follows the divide between the Boundary Waters Canoe Area Wilderness to its south and Quetico to the north. The portage is about three miles from the Cache Bay Ranger Station. On a map, it's found just southwest of the entrance to Quetico heading toward Knife Lake. Leif, who was 11 at the time, still remembers the event with clarity. He and his mom were casually walking along on an otherwise pleasant summer day when a moose lumbered across the portage in front of them. As is the case with most moose showing aggression toward humans, this female moose—a cow—had a young calf in tow. When the moose first crossed the portage trail, they were 20 yards ahead of Janice and Leif, having just emerged from shallow water nearby to seek comfort in the trees.

The cow moose did not hesitate as it continued moving forward into the thick timber and away from the surprised but otherwise unshaken mother and son duo. By that time, Janice had seen many moose during her decades in Quetico and before that as a forester, indeed far too many to remember each particular sighting or encounter. Wanting to respect the space that a cow demands when protecting its young, Janice and Leif stepped off the main route of the portage and moved slowly down an adjacent spur trail that intersects the Monument Portage. They waited there. Seconds went by. The forest remained quiet, the distant call of a white-throated sparrow piercing the silence, warning the pair of impending danger. And then, without any signal, the larger moose came barreling down on them from seemingly nowhere.

"That moose somehow snuck down that trail and we, all of a sudden, just felt and heard this immense stomping," Leif recalls. "We turned around and it was just full-bore coming down the trail at us."

Leif followed his instincts and swiftly leapt behind a large cedar tree. Janice did not find any such barriers substantial enough to obstruct a charging moose, settling instead for a small poplar tree to hide behind. The tiny tree was not wide enough to cover the width of her torso let alone stop an 800-pound charging animal. To further deter the moose, Janice began to flail her limbs like a circus clown, yelling with all the gusto she had.

"This all happened in a matter of seconds," Leif recalls. "I peeked out from behind the cedar and saw my mom throwing her arms all around. I thought she was being stomped or attacked at first. Then I realized she was trying to make the moose back down."

Back down it did, but not before rearing up on its two hind legs and standing partially erect like a horse in a Hollywood movie. Typically done as a means to reach greens growing above their normal reach, when a moose stands on its hind legs, they can be more than 13 feet tall, three feet higher than a regulation basketball hoop. Leif was so close to the moose as it turned to retreat from the flailing park ranger that he could see the animal's chest rise and fall as her lungs inhaled and exhaled, grunting as she made her way out of the situation. And just like that, with hardly an indication as to what direction it would ultimately go, the moose was gone.

Years later, Janice commented to me that perhaps the most challenging or awkward part of such an encounter with a wild animal is how to proceed with the rest of the day. Indeed, heading back to Cache Bay that afternoon was not without its tension.

"Walking back to the landing where our canoe was sitting was just as scary as when the moose was coming right at us," Leif recalls. "Every little sound we heard, we thought for sure was the moose coming back to us."

Ever the teacher, Janice seized the moment as an educational tool, and, perhaps, to justify the experience.

"See how protective moms are of their kids?" she said to Leif.

Leif was present for another encounter involving a charging moose—though it was only viewed by Janice's eyes. When Janice was five months pregnant and just beginning her fourth season at Cache Bay, instead of Leif along for another game of hide-behind-the-tree, that afternoon, Ingela, fresh into her fourth year of life, experienced her first moose encounter. She had been on the island four years now. It was just a matter of time. Janice again noted to me the speed at which this mother moose charged, again without any indication of oncoming hostility.

"Ingela and I were walking away from the ranger station on the far side of the island, and just like that," Janice said, snapping her fingers for emphasis, "there is a moose coming at us."

Ingela's first reaction was to let rip, as Janice described it, "a primordial scream."

"I was looking down at the moss thinking something very heavy has walked here," Janice said. "Next thing I know, Ingela leapt from the ground onto my torso and clung to me, just screaming. The moose was only one body length away from us with its calf walking under the cow's belly."

Now it was both park ranger and moose, mothers protecting their young. Ultimately, both parties split in opposite directions and everyone escaped unharmed. Janice said that, after the encounter, it took some convincing to get Ingela to walk to the outhouse because the cow would often be feeding on shrubs. For a while after, her mother would have to continually clap her hands calling, "Hey, moose, time to go," whenever Ingela was using the restroom or she wouldn't go.

"That made for a long start to the summer," Janice said.

Despite the fact that no one she knew had been physically harmed by the animals, moose are almost indescribably intimidating in a situation like that, Janice pointed out.

"I mean, they are very scary when they are aggressive like this, but it's all part of the bush. This is what life is like for them," she said. "They have to be aggressive to defend their young. It's instinct. I try to educate my campers about these types of things that can happen."

Though somewhat common in Quetico, moose are far from the only animals to have made life interesting for Janice and her family at the Cache Bay Ranger Station. There were plenty of howling wolves, visits from otters, abundant birds, and even a bear that was lucky enough to take in the view of the bay from a large branch near the cabin. And, of course, more than any other animal, there were the scores of two-legged paddlers passing through on their way to or from an adventure in Quetico.

According to park records, the years under Janice's watch from 1985 to 1997 were the busiest on record for the Cache Bay Ranger Station. In recent years, Canadian numbers passing through her station fell. Many of the paddlers now came from the United States, traveling up the Gunflint Trail and then entering the park via Saganaga. These are dedicated paddlers who longed for the remoteness Quetico offers, some claiming that its solitude is a notch higher than that of the nearby Boundary Waters.

Dave Elder, the superintendent who hired Janice to work at the Cache Bay Ranger Station in 1985, made sure their first two years at the park went as smoothly as possible. He and the other park staff knew Janice and Peter were inexperienced when it came to day-to-day life inside the park. The new rangers did not know many of the Americans important to the station, either those who lived locally on Saganaga or those paddlers who visited on a recurring basis. Like a new bartender at a pub full of regulars, trust is established over time. And yet, despite needing to hold the newbie pair's hands, Elder saw greatness in Janice right away. He appreciated her interest in the history of the park and her existing knowledge of the wilds of northwestern Ontario. On paper, Janice was the right choice for the job, and upon his retirement two years later, Elder remained confident he'd selected the right person. That confidence remains unshaken.

"It was apparently a good fit, as she is still there," Elder told me in 2019.

Elder, and nearly every other Quetico employee with whom I talked to about Matichuk, readily set into a confident commentary about her years in the park. The words *dedicated* and *knowledgeable* appeared over and over again, an homage to the longest serving ranger in the history of the park.

Hard work aside, Elder said he appreciates that Matichuk's fascination with her surroundings always kept pace with the many canoe campers who pass through each summer, no matter how many seasons had passed. He observed that it wasn't just the iconic animals of the North— moose, wolf, or bear—that piqued the interest of Matichuk; it was the system working in concert that did it for her.

"She always looked forward to the hatching of the common mergansers that nested under the station buildings every year," Elder said. "She would report the safe journey of the ducklings to the mother duck calling to them at the shoreline."

After more than three decades at the helm, it is unfathomable for those who pass through the checkpoint to think that someone else has ever lived there other than Janice and her family. However, there was another who resided inside the cabin before Matichuk. Throughout my conversations, I heard this time period referred to as the *P.J.* era of the park. This *pre-Janice* reference is not lacking in its biblical intimation.

Among those who previously dwelled on the island, noteworthy is Jon Nelson, a renowned author and historian who currently lives in Thunder Bay. The Nelsons, Jon accompanied by his wife, were the last rangers to live and work a paddling season at Cache Bay prior to Janice and Peter's arrival in 1985.

"I'd heard about Janice long before I ever met her—as had many of us in the park at that time," Nelson told me on a brutally windy November day near the shore of Lake Superior. "I think I first heard of her when she was in Sweden doing forestry work over there. Even then she was building a reputation as someone who knew the area and was a tremendous worker."

Nelson—who is steeped in knowledge related to Quetico's history, its abundant plant and animal life, and the inner workings of the park—said Janice showed dedication and ambition even before she arrived to the island.

"I first met her and Peter at park headquarters in the spring of 1985, just as Marie and I were leaving Cache Bay and switching over to the ranger station at Prairie Portage," Nelson said. "Janice really wanted to know about the history of the park, the native history, and the plants and animals in the park. She wanted to know everything from top to bottom, and Marie and I really appreciated that."

In addition to working as a ranger in the 70s and 80s at several remote outposts within the park, Nelson is also a learned historian of it. To this day, few are as well-versed in the dynamics of Quetico Provincial Park as Nelson is. His 2009 book, *Quetico: Near to Nature's Heart*, makes this clear. In it, he writes of his own experiences at Cache Bay, good times and bad, exciting and not. One particular highlight came from turning just one such slow time into intrigue. From the comforts of his canoe on Saganaga's Swamp Bay, a small inlet not far from the ranger station, Nelson donned homemade imitation moose antlers and was able to coax a moose to the shoreline using a series of moose calls. Upon seeing the creature that was making the sounds—Nelson, floating 20 yards from shore—the moose turned and casually trotted back to the woods from which it came.

"Even back then, there were slow times," Nelson said. "You have to think of things to do every once in a while to mix things up a bit."

When the Nelsons passed the figurative Cache Bay torch to Peter and Janice, they were traveling with two young children of their own, even including a son named Leif.

"Having young children at a ranger station is a terrific experience," Nelson told me. "I have wonderful memories of our two playing in the sandbox at Cache Bay, swinging on the tire swing, fishing and diving from the dock, catching toads, having breakfast with chipmunks, and other things like that."

Within the intense isolation of the Quetico region, communication with friends and family can be a challenge. To offset this, Janice and Nelson's wife, Marie, often chatted over the park radios, at least during their time of overlap in the late 1980s and early 90s. For hours during the long summer nights, they would share stories of motherhood, if for no other reason than to pass the time. Mind you, this was a general use radio frequency, and so story time got to be enjoyed by not just the young mothers, but also by conservation officers making their rounds and other rangers working throughout the park. On occasion, the discussions between Janice, Marie, and another young mother working at the Beaverhouse Ranger Station, Carrie, would veer into less comfortable waters. Jon recalled that some topics could make one squeamish, at least for the men who happened to be listening.

"Sometimes they would start to discuss breastfeeding, getting really in-depth about weaning off, or just talking for extended periods of time about infants in general," Nelson said with a laugh. "I learned later that some of the men listening started scanning the dial for a country music station or just anything else they could find on the radio on nights like those."

Another couple Janice built a strong relationship with in those early years was Joe and Vera Meany. From 1971 to 1996, the Meanys ran the ranger station at Lac la Croix, a Quetico station also on the American border but at the far southwest edge of the park. Joe was an extremely talented canoeist and a marvelous storyteller. His paddle routes across Quetico and throughout greater Canada are the stuff of legend. It is commonly said that Meany was part of a paddling duo that paddled from Ely to Atikokan and, after only one day's rest, back to Ely. They accomplished this faster than anybody ever has, or likely ever will, at least according to Nelson. Indeed,

Meany's reputation among the paddling community has been cemented in the history books by Jon, and there even is a portage trail named after him within Quetico. According to Nelson, it is a terribly challenging portage leading from Alice Lake to Fern Lake, and it is known as the "Sauvage Portage," after Joe Meany and his "sauvage" paddling escapades.

However accomplished he was as a paddler, to Janice, Leif, and Ingela, Joe Meany is best remembered for his riddles. They would arrive with regularity, sometimes over the park radio, other times in more creative ways, Matichuk said. "There's a float plane that arrives once a week with various supplies. One time, off the plane came a present for Ingela. It was a wooden ornament, a slab of pine about a foot long with a three-forked branch underneath that are the legs. On the face of the pine slab is Joe's handwriting and a riddle." The riddle on the pine read:

> *Roty Tote Tote*
> *a little fat man, in a bright red coat,*
> *With a staff in his hand*
> *and a stone in his belly.*
> *You tell me that riddle and I'll give you a penny."*

On the bottom of the wooden treasure, Joe printed:

> *To Ingela at Cache Bay. From Joe at Lac La Croix.*

"I have that gift from Joe sitting at Cache Bay in

the cabin to this day, and campers continue to guess what the riddle is about," Janice said. "Some just recite the poem to me and then ask for a penny. Then I inform them they must guess the riddle."

"What's the answer to the riddle?" I asked after also being stumped.

"A cherry!" Janice said with a laugh.

Prior to the Nelsons, another couple worked together at the Cache Bay Ranger Station in the late 1970s named Holly and Bob Rupert, and before them, a man named John Bouchard worked at the station, starting in 1967. Each person, duo, or family has left their own mark on the island and its pieces over the years. Holly, for example, collected and dried a variety of plants from across the island for decor. She then used a thin plastic coating to attach the plants to a cabin window. Some 40 years later, these same plants still hang sun-kissed but otherwise undisturbed inside the ranger station.

Nelson said that for all the secrets and stories Janice could tell about Quetico, she also had a keen ear. Those last few years were equal parts personal experience and shared experience, brought by paddlers passing through that made her knowledge of the park both historical and current. Janice could tell you where the best campsite was in 1985 or any year after. She knew when the water was high, where a beaver had flooded a portage from, or where the bugs are bad on any given night from May to September. All of this knowledge is not superficial or just to showcase her understanding of the park; it's about keeping people safe and helping them.

Despite the accolades hanging on her wall, Matichuk did not make it a point to highlight her various rescues and heroic acts. While conversing with canoeists entering the park, she did not shy away from talking specifics on safety, but rarely did she use scare tactics to get paddlers to follow the rules or behave reasonably. There was one exception to this, however. The Falls Chain, just northeast of Cache Bay, is a notoriously hazardous stretch of water. Nelson said Matichuk made quick understanding of this during her first days on the job.

"Cache Bay Ranger Station can be difficult to get to and leave from on windy days, and rangers at the station have to be very aware of that. They often have binoculars to watch people coming and going," Nelson said. "In the 1980s, most canoeists were using Fisher Maps that had portages marked incorrectly, some on the wrong side of falls and rapids. This could lead to tragedy in the spring with high water."

It was fortunate that Janice was an excellent canoeist, only surpassed in importance and skill by her instinct. Nelson attested to this even prior to her arrival. She was inherently aware of the value of making sure people were shown where the portages were located and taught not to blindly follow their maps.

"Many of the outfitters had already made the corrections, but others had not. We felt comfortable moving in knowing that Janice was aware of the importance of keeping canoeists as safe as possible,"

Nelson said.

As it goes for anyone who spends a career working in a position where guests come and go, a certain chemistry begins to develop between hosts and their patrons. This unfolds whether one is a librarian, nurse, cashier, or indeed, a ranger at the Cache Bay Ranger Station.

Ken Koscik is a canoe builder who lives near Madison, Wisconsin. Koscik has visited Quetico Park for more than 50 consecutive years, his first trip to the park in 1968. Koscik and his paddling companions—either his immediate family or a handful of his friends—make a point to chat with the interior rangers of Quetico during their annual visits. Koscik said they got to know the Nelsons quite well over those early years, often bringing them a pie or other treats from civilization. Then one day, during their 1985 trip to Quetico, there was suddenly a new face greeting them in Cache Bay. "I walked up to hand the pie to Jon or Marie and there's this new person behind the desk, so I handed the pie to her and said, 'It's yours.' That was Janice and we've been friends ever since," Koscik said with a laugh.

In between the paddling, working, and conversing with paddlers, the common parts of life happened. Janice and Peter watched Ingela and Leif grow from infants to toddlers to teenagers, much of it on the island.

During the offseason, the family would return

1,000 miles to the east, to their remote home on Tilden Lake. There, Ingela and Leif did most of their formal schooling. Education was a part of everyday life on the island, though, the natural world a teacher of its own when humans aren't calling the shots. And when they weren't learning from nature, books were the most basic means of passing the time, a superb source for both education and entertainment. And indeed, without television or video games, there was ample time to read.

"Our parents made a point of reading multiple books to us every night," Ingela said. And once her books were done for the night, the fun didn't end. "If I was lucky, I could stay between my mom and dad while they read their novels, so I could read along."

On one particularly quiet night inside the station, Ingela was situated on the couch with her father on her left and her mother on her right. As she often did, Ingela would peer over their forearms and read their books as her parents turned their pages.

"At one point, my dad saw me looking around the room and asked if I was bored of the story," Ingela said. "I told him no, I was just waiting for him to change the page."

Peter, curiosity with his young daughter piqued, said he had been under the impression that Ingela was reading along with Janice's book, not the one he held in his hands. Ingela acknowledged that she indeed was reading her mother's book. In fact, Ingela said, she was also waiting for her mom to turn the page. Both Janice and Peter now paused and looked skeptically at each other. Testing their daughter's honesty, Janice and Peter requested a summary of what was happening in each respective book. Without hesitation, Ingela gave a succinct report of each story, with details specific to each plot, current to the exact page they were on.

"I had a better grasp of Dad's book than he did," Ingela said lightheartedly, some 25 years after the moment occurred.

Ingela and Leif rarely lacked creative tasks and spontaneous adventures on the island as well. In addition to relatively basic activities like swimming, exploring, and fishing, Janice proudly thought of her daughter as a highly capable "mini-ranger" throughout her growing up. Leif, too, was interactive with visitors to the park. He brought a well-practiced routine to the office where paddlers obtained permits, pulling pranks on unwary campers. Janice wasn't immune to getting roped in to his shenanigans.

"Mom and I had it worked out where she knew I would be down there and would talk extra-long and animatedly to distract them," Leif said. "I would tie their laces to the leg under the desk, or tie the laces of the two shoes together. I tended to get mixed reactions from people, but we thought it was great."

On an island located entirely within a cherished and protected wilderness, there's not much in the way of cycling or organized-sports. Instead, the children grew up to be comfortable in canoes in the way most kids grow up riding bikes or shooting baskets in the driveway. Life for the children on the island was all about learning to keep themselves entertained with what was available, namely books, young visitors on family trips, and of course, the natural world.

It could be said that a direct link to nature, an escape from pavement, and spectacular solitude are the key ingredients that many paddlers are in pursuit of when they come to Quetico. However, it's these same characteristics that made life challenging for the two children growing up on their mother's island in the park.

"It could be very lonely and boring on the island sometimes," Ingela told me one day. "Sure, we were out there in God's country, but our parents were running an office, on the job from eight to five and often later."

What this meant, Ingela explained, was that she and her brother would take nearly every opportunity to interact with visitors to Cache Bay. Because of these interactions, and despite the obstacles that came from living for half of each year surrounded by wilderness, Ingela is quick to recall the many friendships that the family forged on the island.

Among those cherished friends are Wisconsin residents John and Julie Rose.

The Roses first met Janice and her family in 1985 during Janice's first year working in the park. Julie said the solitude and nature of Quetico were the draws for her and John to visit annually from their home in Chicago, but over the years, visiting the family that lived at the Cache Bay Ranger Station became an essential part of every trip north.

"We actually started leaving the interior and racing through the portages so that we could spend more time with Janice and Peter," Julie said. "Over time, the children continued to be a part of our visits and occasions for joy."

John remembers fishing with both Leif and Ingela from the time they were barely old enough to hold a fishing rod, let alone tie a lure to their lines. In time, John became that trusted visitor that the kids knew would always be primed for an adventure. Julie would often stay behind and visit with Janice while the others went fishing. On one particular day, while Janice was busy in the office, Julie went down to the dock to greet Ingela, Leif, and John as they returned from a traipse through the park. As she walked along the large wooden causeway that greets arriving canoeists, she slipped and fell straight into the water.

"I remember I came out of the freezing water and Ingela started to cry," Julie said, adding that seeing her cry made her feel yet worse. After drying off, it was explained to Ingela and Leif that Julie had only slipped and that the tumble was an accident. It was another teaching opportunity for Janice, about why one needs to know how to swim, how to rescue yourself, and that ultimately, sometimes bad things happen unexpectedly .

Both Ingela and Leif spent 16 summers on that island. Naturally, the family has a mixture of emotions and memories about their time there. Being surrounded by what some consider to be the most beautiful natural setting on the planet did not remove the family from the complex dynamics involved in relationships. Some of the memories remain unsettled for the family. Over time, Janice and Peter's differences grew past reconciliation. It was time to move on.

The couple divorced after the 1997 season and Peter never returned to the island. Janice found herself alone on her island and faced with an uncertain future. There would be bills to pay. The work was now all hers. Taking a deep breath, she started this new journey with a look in the mirror.

She was terrified at what she saw.

Janice and Leif, 1998

Janice and Ingela

*Janice teaches a group of paddlers about the surrounding
Quetico Wilderness, 1994*

Janice in her element inside the ranger station

Janice's goal was to get to know her guests on a personal level, beyond just the trip's details

Janice radios a nearby Quetico station

Both experienced and novice groups to Quetico often inquire about various routes with Janice

Janice presents to a group of canoe campers

Cache Bay Outhouse

Water tanks at the Cache Bay Ranger Station

Janice's birthday, 2007

Chapter Five
The Dark Side of the Island

"Do you not see how necessary a world of pains and troubles is to school an intelligence and make it a soul?"
—John Keats, *Letters of John Keats*

Despite the idyllic world in which Janice lived, there were certainly times that were troubled. Just last summer, she suffered a severe injury. The way Janice Matichuk described it, one moment, her finger was there, fully capable of pointing with whatever index appendage she preferred. An instant later, it was gone.

Throughout our time together, I am half-surprised that not once did I get another finger pointed my way, literally or figuratively. Perhaps there were times it seemed she would have liked to. It happens when you dig into the details of someone's life. Even though my explicit purpose was to tell her *whole* story, Janice treated me as she would any other paddler. What Matichuk did do for me, and thousands of other curious paddlers who entered through Cache Bay at some point during the past 35 years, was point me in the right direction. When

Matichuk pointed you where to go, you went there. No questions asked.

At approximately 11:45 a.m. on August 24, 2019, pointing the way became a little more difficult. A plane carrying two canoeists arrived at the Cache Bay Ranger Station.

"When campers drive to Atikokan here in Ontario and use a local outfitter, they can fly to Cache Bay and commence their trip from my dock," Matichuk explained to me in November, 2019. "They then paddle across the entire width of Quetico back toward Atikokan and exit at the north end. Thus the plane."

The pilot, a well-seasoned navigator of the airspace above Quetico, had just landed the aircraft and taxied the travelers to Matichuk's dock like he had a thousand times before. The scene was all quite routine and it was an otherwise beautiful morning in the park. Light winds carried the dry smell of centuries-old pines. Sunbeams slid across tiny ripples on the water surrounding the island. The only sound other than loons and the occasional songbird was that of the float plane's engine, droning throughout the bay. Matichuk went to the dock to greet those on board as the plane touched down.

Dressed in her standard attire—navy blue shorts that ended just above the knee and a park-issued collared, khaki shirt—Matichuk approached the plane to extend welcoming words to the canoe campers. She waited for the plane's propeller to stop spinning on the large, fixed wooden dock that stretches out from the shoreline of the island, and once it had, walked out onto a floating extension that goes another 15 feet out. Though the prop had stopped, the plane was still in a guided drift, the pilot controlling rudders in the water at the back of each float. As the plane neared its target, Matichuk lifted a heavy, thick rope used for tying down water- or air-craft upon their arrival. She knew exactly where she was going to affix the rope to the plane, but when she reached for that spot, a cleat at the front of the float was occupied by a rope holding the canoe tight to the plane. This forced her to change her plan; all the while, the craft remained in motion. Matichuk moved her right hand between the taut canoe rope and the plane, passing the dock rope around the strut to her left hand. Then, the way she described it, one moment her finger was there, still fully able to point; the next, it was gone.

Matichuk said it was a perfect storm sort of situation. As Janice brought the rope to a different cleat with her left hand, her right remained on the strut, holding on to the plane. In a blink, the dock rope went taut as it caught the plane's momentum, her right hand suddenly stuck under the tension of the rope and the slow movement of the heavy plane. Her finger *briefly* bore the entirety of the plane's inertia. It had no chance. And so off it came.

"The next thing I knew, my right index finger was amputated and lying there in the palm of my hand," Matichuk calmly said. "No pain, very little blood."

Naturally, a burst of activity ensued. Matichuk

immediately shoved her amputated finger back onto the remaining stump and sprinted to the ranger station. Two campers helped wrap her hand in gauze. She could well have put it in her pocket, but instead, she literally kept it *on-hand*. She certainly made sure to keep track of it.

Voice shaking, Matichuk contacted park headquarters over the radio. It was determined that the plane that had just inadvertently cut Janice's finger off would serve as an air ambulance. The freshly arrived canoeists, dumbstruck by what was unfolding, were instructed to start their trip and figure out the permits and fees later. The ranger station was closed up and locked. Matichuk got on board the plane and closed her eyes, all while holding her hand across her chest and upon her shoulder.

"This was important for me to do—otherwise, it would have started bleeding severely," Matichuk said. "Actually, I kept it up higher than my heart for 13 hours. First aid training from when I was a Brownie paid off, once again."

Forty minutes after her finger was sliced free, she landed some 65 miles away on Eva Lake, on the north side of Quetico. Kashabowie Outposts, a small seaplane base, is located there and an ambulance was waiting to transport Matichuk 22 miles to the hospital in Atikokan. Time was crucial if Matichuk had any hope of keeping her finger. She did her best to stay calm, continuing to hold her hand up high, pacing her breathing.

At the hospital in Atikokan, the first medical

professional to examine Janice's finger was not optimistic. After the gauze was unwound, Matichuk made the mistake of looking down at the splint she'd made to keep her finger in place.

"Everything was gray and purple," she said. "And the doctor made a noise that I didn't think boded well for the finger."

Once it was determined that the situation would require a specialist, the hospital directed Matichuk by plane to a special amputee hospital in London, Ontario, about 90 minutes southwest of Toronto and approximately 1,000 miles away from Atikokan. She arrived roughly 13 hours after the injury occurred, by necessity, the multi-hour reattachment procedure starting almost immediately.

Janice was not put under for the entirety of the surgery. At one point, Matichuk's finger and upper hand were strategically frozen using specialized equipment, a source of "crazy pain," Matichuk said.

And then it was over.

The next morning, five hours after the surgery ended, medical staff unwrapped the bandages and reviewed their work.

"My finger looked dead. It was now black, or a dark purple. It was swollen and mangled," Matichuk said.

If the past 24 hours hadn't been strange enough, a team of doctors then cut off Matichuk's fingernail and applied leeches to the wounded finger, one leech every hour for the next 48 consecutive hours. The leeches slowly fulfilled their purpose, keeping blood circulating through the imperiled finger while allowing the body to slowly get the tiny veins in her surgically repaired finger back in sync with the rest of its surroundings.

Matichuk kept her eyes closed much of that time. She thought about Cache Bay and the canoe campers she sent off without her guidance. She thought about her children. Matichuk remained in the hospital for eight more days before going home.

There was much to sort out. With her finger wrapped in heavy bandaging, Matichuk knew her season in Quetico was done. It could've been worse; the ranger station was closing in a few short weeks anyway. Still, Matichuk needed to get back to the island. She had possessions she wanted for the winter, items to take home, food to get out of the cabin. Never in the previous 34 years had she left so abruptly, and she couldn't stand for it.

Nearly three weeks after surgery, Matichuk was able to get back to Cache Bay for a "hurried and mostly chaotic" trip to the island. Other park staff had been assigned to help finalize the closure of the ranger station. Matichuk was strictly there to grab the few items she needed. There was nothing sentimental or enjoyable about the process, let alone time enough to come to peace with the trauma.

She returned to Atikokan with her finger in tatters and an exhausting recovery process just barely started. And yet, despite her recent down luck, in November without fail, Matichuk was once again faced with two familiarities: Winter and depression.

Depression does not care about amputated fingers. It doesn't care if you're a man or a woman. And it doesn't matter if you are the longest serving ranger in the history of Quetico Provincial Park. "It's like being possessed by an evil demon," Matichuk told me of her longstanding bouts with depression. "It can take control of your life."

I asked her to describe how she felt when depression took over. Her response was three words: "Hopeless. Lifeless. Overwhelmed."

How and why could someone in her position—idolized, hard-working, motivated, lifesaving, seemingly fearless park ranger—get bogged down with something like depression?

"The truth is, there's no easy answer," explained Sherri Moe, a licensed psychotherapist who specializes in anxiety, depression, and trauma. One factor that could have played a role was the cumulative pressure of Matichuk's job itself. When six canoeists capsized and Matichuk was able to rescue five, an enormous amount of pressure was generated, and the story of what happened to Tom Ackerman that day is just one day, one example.

"A lot of professionals in emergency medicine, backcountry firefighters, someone working a job like Janice's; they need to deal with the aftereffects of what has happened," Moe said. "Cumulatively, you're talking a lot of experiences that she has helped people through. Now, that hasn't maybe been about her individually, but that weight has been put on her. That accumulation of all these stressors and people's responses. Pain, injury, fear, and struggle. She carries that for people to make *them* feel okay. But then what does she do to get rid of it?"

Matichuk was diagnosed with clinical depression in her early 40s. It took her years to accept this diagnosis. Though she took prescription medication for 23 years after being formally diagnosed, she disclosed to me that she despised the "dullness" that the medicine "brought to everything."

Fast forward to her glioblastoma diagnosis and her reaction was almost the opposite. "I never went into a denial phase. Cancer is something I could accept, believe it or not. It makes me angry, but I never had denial about it. Depression was harder for me to accept. It was for many years."

Matichuk was willing to accept the fact that the highs and lows of her profession likely played a role in her depression over the years. For one thing, she was a seasonal employee, only on the island for part of the year. From October through April, Matichuk was technically unemployed. Her last few years, Matichuk spent her winters in a modest home in a residential part of Atikokan. With temperatures often plunging far below zero for days or even weeks in a row, social interaction could be quite limited, and living so far north, there is a physiological effect from the lack of sunlight, so it isn't exactly surprising that the off-seasons were hard on Janice.

"It's more profound in the winter," Matichuk explained of her depression, "because I don't have as much distraction."

Her last winter was particularly challenging. Between her seasonally amplified depression, rehabilitation to her finger, and the collective sense of fear from the coronavirus pandemic, it all added up to perhaps her most uncertain paddling season since her divorce.

"I'm having just a devil of a time," Matichuk told me in March, 2020, about two months before she was scheduled to return to the ranger station. A month later came the cancer diagnosis. As it went for many in 2020, bad news kept compounding. Darkness on darkness. Waters too treacherous to navigate. All of it very real.

Though she often thought of it as her sanctuary, Matichuk admitted to many days on the island where depression crept in on her. Throughout the past decade, there were nights when Matichuk went to sleep still wearing her park uniform, the thought of putting on pajamas becoming an unsurmountable obstacle. "Even if I didn't physically work hard that day, I would just be exhausted. I would go to bed at 6:30 p.m., too done in to even take off my clothes," she said. "So I'd just go to bed in the uniform and get up and start the next day with the same clothes on. It's difficult for someone to imagine how depression can own your soul."

She was always able to mask her emotions from visitors and excited canoeists who were just starting their trip to Quetico, she told me, even in those days of utter darkness. "I can perform my job for campers.

But as soon as they leave, my shoulders sag down again, I get to feeling tired again, the whole thing cycles back through. I can always pull it together for others, but not myself."

Often the trouble of mental health struggles are their inconsistency. It would certainly be worse to be depressed one hundred percent of the time, but the fall from high to low makes one keenly aware of what is missing when in a state of retreat. Depression aside, Janice couldn't make it more clear that the good days at Cache Bay far outweighed the bad. She loved her job and in many ways lived for it.

This is not unusual, Moe explained. "Cache Bay was her solace, or her remedy, so to say."

Few would question whether the physical act of rescuing canoeists, caring for sick or injured guests in the park, and the necessity of remaining constantly vigilant over everything happening within a large, untamed wilderness can create a strain over time. And indeed it certainly may have amplified Matichuk's condition, but she believed her bouts of struggle with mental health started far before she ever donned a park uniform. She thought that it went back to the fifth grade, around when she took on her first role with responsibility, as crossing guard. "That's what started all this. I remember becoming very earnest and determined that day," Matichuk said with a laugh.

Matichuk confided in me that she didn't necessarily think that her new job at the time caused her depression, per se. Instead, her memory of the school principal assigning the crossing-guard duties might perhaps have been the moment in time that stands out as a turning point. Moe seems to agree with this latter, more wholistic interpretation, thinking that it was likely her brain chemistry was charted for troubled waters long before she was chosen to help students safely cross the street.

"It's an early recollection," Moe said of the crossing-guard story that Matichuk cited to me as a turning point. "We each have them and they're not an experience that would be traumatic, necessarily. It's just that we have something that clicks in us that says, 'This is my role in the world.' It gives us a sense of identity, but also of confidence. Maybe at that age, she had been searching, wondering what her role was. She was probably wondering about that, and then all of a sudden, Janice was the crossing guard, and she had a purpose."

Moe and others in her field often point out that every human, particularly at a young age, wants to know three things: 1) that they are safe; 2) that they are significant; and 3) that they belong. The role of a crossing guard, much like that of a being a park ranger on an island in the wilderness for more than three decades, provided a direct path to all three of these desires.

Acquiring and maintaining these preferred states can be exhausting, particularly for someone like Matichuk, who was attempting to keep not just herself safe, significant, and belonging, but also those around her. Moe connects this notion to Janice's struggle throughout winter 2019-20.

"That's tough, especially when you're the one who is supposed to be keeping everyone safe," Moe said. "It's like, you're the crossing guard and you yourself just got hit by the car."

Interwoven with the parts of Matichuk's depression that were more predictable were the circumstantial elements. When your finger gets sliced off and ends up in the palm of your hand, trauma is expected to surface. Add on terminal brain cancer, and one's psyche plunges to new depths.

Whenever Matichuk was faced with either cyclical or circumstantial depression, she typically escaped from it through work. During the winter months away from her island, Matichuk volunteered frequently for the Beaten Path Nordic Ski Club in Atikokan, cutting brush from trails. She helped out a number of other nonprofits as well, including the Friends of Quetico and the Atikokan Pictograph Art Gallery.

All of this isn't to say that Matichuk's challenges weren't without their benefits. She was dedicated and engaged to an extreme degree, certain to have optimized her role in every way. It should come as no surprise that in addition to her incessant hard work, Matichuk was also a perfectionist, and she held those around her to the same high standards she did herself. Ingela told me that her mother had two gears: "On and working or off and flat-lined."

"She instilled a work ethic in me that I am trying to tame," Ingela said. "Work ethic and workaholic are interchangeable for both of us. I've been trying to understand why her, my grandparents, and I work the way we do, to the bone, with no regard for our own lives. It could very well be simple addiction."

Being addicted to work was not a sentiment Matichuk shied away from. She knew that she pushed too hard on occasion, demanding too much from herself. This level of expectation certainly played a role in the continual highs and lows she felt each year. Depression. Physical therapy. Brain cancer. In Matichuk's final year, she had been dealt a tough hand. She told me that where once she thought she could simply think her way into good health, or use her intelligence and drive to simply move forward, time had proven otherwise, for better or worse.

"A psychiatrist in North Bay once told me that my depression has nothing to do with willpower," Matichuk said. "That what I have is a chemical imbalance in my brain. I remember that conversation very clearly. She told me that people with depression are high functioning, very creative, and often very hardworking people. That was significant, even though you can find that on the Internet anywhere nowadays, or read it in a book. It was important for me to hear that from a person talking directly to me."

Moe said there are universal truths to what depression is, various influences upon symptoms and cycle, and how it affects people at different stages of their lives. Nobody asks to have lows, to be anhedonic, just as they don't ask for brain cancer. Sickness, both mental and physical, arrive and take their grip, often with little explanation. The playbook is simple for diagnosis: you have it or you don't. Study of the condition is further troubled by the inherently relative nature of data about it. One cannot easily and objectively record the pathology of someone experiencing depression.

Moe is tall, athletic, and accustomed to working hard herself. She lives in a remote outpost near Minnesota's Arrowhead Trail where, in addition to being a psychotherapist, she teaches yoga and helps run a sled-dog operation. Her husband, Frank, is a well-known musher and environmentalist who once served in Minnesota's House of Representatives. When Moe talks about Matichuk, she is spirited, though deliberate, carefully choosing her words, a habit of her profession or a sign of respect for the Quetico park ranger; likely, a combination of both.

When Moe crossed paths with Matichuk in Grand Marais at the 2013 Dragon Boat Festival on the shores of Lake Superior, she was taken aback by how popular the isolated ranger from Quetico was around town. It was instantly clear to Moe that Matichuk had an influential presence in Grand Marais and the border communities at large. "Matichuk is recognized as a ranger first and foremost," Moe said, "but also for her varied appearances at the North House Folk School and their seasonal celebrations and community dances. People know her here. She's recognized by a lot of people when she comes to town."

Among those who looked forward to seeing Matichuk each and every trip into town was her longtime friend and paddling partner Bonnie Schudy. Though most of her stories focus on the adventurous spirit of her friend, Schudy admitted that Matichuk was not "the superhero or superwoman that, on the surface, she seemed to be." Still, tears began to flow down Schudy's cheeks as she described how much she admired her friend's perseverance, her incredible endurance and energy when in service of others.

"I look at her and I admire her so much. Her life. Everything in her life," Schudy said, pausing to gather herself. "As my husband says when she spends the night at our house, 'It seems like Janice has this dark cloud following her.' But she gets through that dark cloud and finds the silver lining in anything and anyone. And that's just a great trait to have."

I spoke to countless people about Matichuk over the course of nearly two years and almost everyone echoed similar sentiments. They would say she was a character almost larger than life, and yet at her core, she revealed the same painful truths that sit with everyone by *at most* one degree of separation. Ultimately, it may be the act of exposing this darkness that she carried that will be her greatest contribution. By opening this view of her flaws, Matichuk wanted to make it okay for others to admit they too weren't perfect. Braving a fierce storm on the unforgiving waters of Saganaga Lake to save a life was indeed courageous. Admitting she had blemishes, speaking openly of her depression, fighting terminal disease with courage; these were perhaps Matichuk's most heroic feats.

Every summer, Matichuk hauled a fresh round of art supplies with her when she returned to the Cache Bay Ranger Station. The creative outlets provided her an escape from the dark spaces in her mind. She lamented that, too often, she failed to utilize them. "Some years, I didn't even get around to opening the boxes with paint or things that I brought out to work on to try to keep busy at night," she said. "Even though I know it's important and would make me feel better, I just can't seem to get around to doing it. Depression freezes me."

Matichuk remained a human being who suffered from mental illness despite the accolades that hung upon her wall. It had been with her since she was very young, and continued to be until she took her final breath.

In one of our last conversations, she made clear that some people's attitude about depression pained her. "When my brain malfunctions, I have no control over it. When people tell me to 'just think positive' or 'think your way out of it' and that kind of stuff, it makes me just want to smack something," Matichuk said. "I wouldn't tell someone to think their way out of high cholesterol or diabetes. What I have is a brain disease. A lot of people have it, and really, it's nothing we need to feel ashamed about anymore."

While depression was a constant companion, Matichuk's outlook held steadfast with the cancer diagnosis. She understood the cruel tragedy of having two separate brain diseases, laughing at her luck. Her brain was her best tool and her worst enemy. "This damn thing up here," she said, pointing with a crippled index finger toward her head.

On two separate occasions in recent years, Janice's experience with depression had made full circles. Each time, a small group of canoe campers visiting Quetico happened to paddle past Matichuk on a day-trip away from the ranger station. They were on the months-long routes, and after getting to know the groups and talking about their trips, each in turn revealed that they were there for a specific reason: to better understand their own depression. Getting away from the busy world and more in touch with nature was a means for them to find a new peace with their clinical depression. How Matichuk found them is a mystery to her; she simply happened to be in the right place at the right time.

"Well, didn't we just have a good gab!" Matichuk said enthusiastically. "When people live with depression and meet others with the same, it's like a secret language. They really get it. It's almost exciting because you totally understand each other, unlike any other relationship." She seemed truly pleased that her sanctuary was theirs too.

Contentment is one of the key spices to the good life. This rings true if you're alone on an island in the Canadian wilderness or if you spend your days in a cramped cubicle within a sprawling metro. When it comes to depression, acceptance is key, Moe said, but if Matichuk's strength was what facilitated her highs, what kept her going throughout the lows was a little bit of community, found just across the water of

Saganaga Lake.

Chapter Six
A Community Across the Water

Frank Szatkowski first visited Quetico Provincial Park in 1979. He was six years old at the time. To earn a spot in the canoe on his rookie outing, Frank had to swim a half-mile across a lake without assistance. Once he proved he was up to the task, his father and uncle assured him that a trip to Quetico would be in the works. Fearlessly, Frank channeled his inner Olympian and propelled himself across the pond. The rest is history.

"Once I started going to Quetico, that was it," Frank said. "I knew it was the place I would be going for the rest of my life."

On that first journey north, Frank's youthful curiosities were, naturally, more free to expand. There was sure to be a moose around every turn in the labyrinth of lakes and rivers. Nearly every fish he hooked strained his kid-size fishing rod nearly to its breaking point. The stars at night were like nothing he had ever seen or imagined on this planet. Quetico was a land of endless possibilities, a place where everything—from the trees and walleye to the sparkling skies— seemed larger.

Some 40 years later, Frank is now taking his own children into the remote Ontario park , though not before they, too, prove they are capable swimmers. The purpose of the open-water swim test, in addition to being able to adequately stay afloat, is so that the children can demonstrate that they are mentally and physically prepared for a canoe trip to the wilderness. That standard had not changed since *his* youth. There were many other particulars surrounding these trips that have changed over the years, though. That being the case, since 1985, at least one other feature of the trips had remained the same.

"Throughout all three generations of Szatkowskis traveling to Quetico, one thing has been constant, and that's Ranger Janice," Frank said. "To me, Janice *is* Cache Bay and Quetico. She dedicated herself to protecting this land that has become one of our favorite places on this earth."

Frank, an avid angler who prefers to keep his hair short and his mustache trimmed, lives with his wife Kathy and their four children in a populous area of eastern Wisconsin. The drive to northeastern Minnesota and the Gunflint Trail is nearly nine hours from their home. Very much a family that prefers tradition, they rent their canoes and other equipment from Tuscarora Lodge & Canoe Outfitters near the end of the Gunflint every trip into Quetico. From there, it's another two hours by shuttleboat and canoe before they reach the ranger station at Cache Bay.

"When we arrive, she is there," Frank told me. *She* is, of course, Janice Matichuk.

"Once we get to her office, she reminds us about safety and protecting the park and the wildlife," Frank told me, happy to submit to the due diligence of process required year after year. "She tells us some of her amazing stories about moose and other wildlife, going over the falls in her canoe and most importantly, how she has saved the lives of several paddlers over the years. Her stories never get old."

Stories, both recent experiences and old tales collected throughout the course of life, are a reflection of where a person has been. In a sense, stories are maps showing us who we've met and the events that have shaped us. If you had been lucky enough to spend any amount of time with Matichuk, you would know at least some of the many stories she told about Saganaga Lake and the diverse community of residents and visitors who enjoy it. Indeed, as nearly anyone would attest, Matichuk was neither short on stories nor the ability to tell them.

"She's a bit long-winded sometimes, but usually in the best kind of way," one decades-long friend of Matichuk's told me, anonymously, of course. They hadn't wanted it to get back to Janice, lest she stop sharing so freely.

All the same, it's at Quetico, and particularly on Saganaga Lake, where Matichuk's life formed into the real-life character that many people—from park employees to paddling enthusiasts—looked to as the ultimate ambassador of what the wilderness stands for.

"She has done this by showing professional work ethic, consistent longevity, and caring for the environment and its users," Matichuk's friend Becky Kayser said. "Janice is a strong individual, both physically and mentally, to live in the solitude of Cache Bay. On top of that, she has the soft side, caring deeply about her family, friends, and campers that use Quetico Park."

Paddlers from Minnesota and other states across the Midwest are the most common visitors to Cache Bay, though Matichuk greeted visitors from all 50 states over the years.

As fascinating—and perhaps occasionally long winded—as her stories can be, there's only so much time on any given canoe trip. Janice certainly maximized that interval each paddler would spend at the Cache Bay Ranger Station. Elsewhere, the check-in might have been but a fraction of any journey, perhaps to the chagrin of some. Anxious canoeists travel many hours and hundreds of miles just to visit the park, so the campers can only stick around to chit-chat for so long before the pull of the wilderness returns them to their canoes and away from the ranger station. Thus, each visit with a paddler was exciting, but often short-lived. Following her divorce, and once her kids were old enough to spend their summers away from the island, more and more, Matichuk needed a community. She needed to fill the void left by her departed companions, and as much as the plants and animals had been enough company from childhood through parenthood, they were no longer. Any virgin empty-nester can relate, and the island amplified that feeling. Fortunately, there was a large door just waiting for her to walk through.

The Saganaga community, even on the Canadian side, remains an extension of the Gunflint Trail community, its terminus in fact. In some ways, this is peculiar, given that the iconic roadway sits entirely in Minnesota. Events such as the Gunflint Canoe Race, a fundraiser for the area volunteer fire department, brings this tight-knit community together on an annual basis. Here, friends from iconic lakes along the trail, Gunflint, Seagull, Saganaga, Loon, Poplar, Clearwater, West Bearskin, Hungry Jack, and others, come together for celebration and reunion.

They also band together in tough times. In 2007, the Ham Lake Fire blackened much of the land at the end of the Gunflint and its surroundings. Treasured homes were destroyed in the blaze, including numerous cabins on mighty Sag. Still others were spared through courageous acts, friends and neighbors putting their lives on the line to save each other's property, possessions, and all the memories they helped create. Years later, many of the homes that were damaged by the fire have been rebuilt. Indeed, the Trail community understands all too well the risks that come from living in such a remote environment.

There was an old map of the surrounding area situated on the desk of the main office when Matichuk arrived at the Cache Bay Ranger Station in 1985. It was a classic Fisher-made map, complete with coffee-blurred portage trails and tattered corners. Superficially unimpressive and hardly useful, upon closer inspection, it revealed itself a treasure map—a handful of names were plotted upon it. Art and Dinna Madsen. Charlotte Powell. Tempest and Irv Benson. Matichuk looked at the names and others. She studied them, saying each aloud. Something about those names grabbed her attention. As though she were reading the Dead Sea Scrolls, the words Matichuk said carried a weight. They are the family names of those deeply rooted in Saganaga, homesteaders and survivors.

"I met them all," Matichuk said of the legendary residents of Sag and the end of the Gunflint. "I guess you could say I got in with that old guard. The originals. Even people like Justine Kerfoot down on Gunflint Lake, I met her around that time as well. I got in on the tail end of them."

Matichuk and I discussed them all, and while each was unique in their own way, Matichuk painted Art Madsen as a particularly "colorful character" from the days of yore. He had been a Quetico Ranger during the 1930s, a member of the unit often referred to as *the original* Quetico Rangers. He built the second ranger station in Cache Bay for the park and was intimately familiar with the area that Matichuk would later patrol and cherish for more than three decades. Black and white photographs of Madsen from his early days in Quetico show a lumbering woodsman possessing massive hands and a curious smile. In many of the pictures, there is a pistol on his hip, and a rifle in his hands. Unlike the Boundary Waters Canoe Area Wilderness to the south, firearms are now prohibited in Quetico. Madsen would likely have strong opinions about that notion.

Madsen, who died in 2000, claimed to have visited "every lake in Quetico," of which there are thousands. He also built and operated Camp Sagonto, on Sag, a rustic wilderness camp that operates to this day. Reflecting on the Quetico pioneer, Matichuk said Madsen was always quick to share a good story, intimately familiar with the history of the park and generous with his experience navigating its treasured waters. "He would talk about bears and wolves and outlaw trappers. He had all kinds of wild stories," Matichuk said.

Madsen's legacy on Sag is one of several that will stand forever. Without question, among Madsen's peers are the entire Powell family. They are historically recognizable, part of the Saganaga Lake area bedrock, and have been a mainstay in the region for more than 100 years. Always willing to welcome new faces and new beginnings on the lake, Dick and Sherry Powell were among the first residents Janice met back in 1985.

"The Powells were among the first people outside of the park that I really got to know well," Janice said. "In the 80s and 90s, we would motor down to them just to get off the island and take a break from our front yard. We called the area we would go to 'Downtown Sag.' There's a bunch of islands really close together, many cabins and some amazing people. There's so much history there."

Dick's grandparents were Jack Powell, a resourceful and ambitious fellow who arrived from Scotland via Michigan, and Mary Ottertail, from the Lac La Croix First Nation. Jack and Mary wed in 1901, eventually building a homestead on Saganagons Lake, past the Falls Chain northeast out of Cache Bay. Dick's parents, Bill and Dorothy, opted slightly to the south of Jack and Mary, starting Saganaga's Chippewa Inn fishing outpost in 1959. Dick and Sherry would take over that family business years later. In addition to possessing a family name rich in local history, Dick and Sherry are known for their generosity and sense of humor. They were also among Matichuk's dearest friends. "To me, they kind of define this area," she told me, backing that up with stories of the many times they helped friends, neighbors, or strangers simply because, "It is way people do things around here."

Dick and Sherry, along with countless others, agree that after living in Quetico for over 30 years, Matichuk is a member of that same pantheon, both inside and out of the park boundaries. It's more than time, however, that qualifies Matichuk to be this iconic representative of the park. It's her personality, her presence. When I asked them to describe Matichuk as they saw her, the Powells selected three words without hesitation. "Tough, committed, and brave." It is the fact that these three traits describe her that makes her part of the group. Of course, they could also be applied to the Powells, and indeed the others who choose to call this rugged place their home. It is self-evident that these are the qualifications: if one doesn't exhibit them, they are naturally weeded out, and often rather quickly. But those who do stay become intertwined in this unique group of people. They are traditional, still living a way of life more customary decades or centuries ago. Shaving is done for special occasions rather than as a part of morning routines. It's a place of duality; where the smell of wood smoke can be either soothing or dangerous depending upon its source, the beauty and the peril of the wild is on display, and that sacred silence can be a blessing and a curse.

Many of the homes on Sag are only accessible by water or ice, requiring planning and execution for simple luxuries. Little things like being able to drop by a loved one's house when you're lonely require a bigger commitment. In her solo years at the station, Matichuk would touch base with the residents of the Sag community to curb that isolation. "Sag Radio," to which it is informally referred, is carried out over a separate frequency from official park business, and it became something of an entertainment channel over the years. "We told stories, we talked about the weather, we passed the time," Matichuk said.

A group of cabin dwellers, including Janice when off duty, became familiar voices on Sag Radio. Like a collection of truck drivers sharing conditions and anecdotes from *the road*, the lines told over Sag Radio were full of colorful chatter. Identifying names—radio handles—were part of the fun. During its peak hours, there are some two dozen handles that can be heard on or are listening to Sag Radio at any given time. Among the names decorating the airwaves are Exile, Brown's Island, Cache Bay, Wire Bender, Frostbite Falls, Bad Dog, Wild Man, Fossil, Trading Post, Bluebird, Raven Rock, Two Percent, and Chippewa; the list goes on and on. In a place like this, the radio is their news and their townhall. It is a way to stay in touch with neighbors, even when the nearest front door could be miles away.

"You could figure out where everyone was, what people were doing the following morning or later in the evening. It was like a party line across the lake," Janice said.

On occasion, Matichuk would use Sag Radio for help at Cache Bay. Quetico Park Headquarters are in Atikokan, sixty miles to the north and with a million acres of wilderness in between, and while the park maintenance team always did their best to fix any pressing issue, doing so required securing a bush plane and coordinating staff to fly to Cache Bay. To avoid inconveniencing the staff for relatively small projects or repairs, Matichuk would instead radio various Sag residents to help with things like a leaky waterline or antenna problems. She had people with the expertise to help with electrical issues, others for outdoors pests; Dick Powell was Matichuk's go-to about anything propane or generator-related. "All the advice from the Sag cabin owners assisted me in fixing these issues immediately," Matichuk said.

The Sag community indeed proved vital during her best years at Cache Bay. From 1999 to the 2019, Matichuk had no choice but to immerse herself in the joys of this select, isolated, and strong community. She opened her heart to her friends and neighbors. The domain of her stories ever expanded, from tales of paddling or conditions inside Quetico, to the timeless bond of friendship. After the divorce from Peter and with Leif and Ingela off on their own, it wouldn't be surprising for Janice's passion to have faded. Instead, her work and dedication to the park only grew stronger. She was by herself on the island, but never alone. Supporting her through it all was the community across Sag.

The Gunflint Trail makes its conclusion in a small loop, roughly one thousand feet in diameter. Here, near the Trail's End Campground and several other points of water access, if one intends to go anywhere, their options are to either make the long drive back toward Grand Marais or hop in a vessel. The trail's loop is surrounded on three sides by water: Seagull Lake to the south, Gull Lake to the west, and the mighty Saganaga to the north. The U.S. Forest Service operates a modest campground there, and several canoe outfitters and a resort-turned-museum are located nearby. With no bounds on her community, the business owners on this stretch of the Gunflint were Matichuk's family too.

Among those who were deeply familiar with Matichuk is Sue Prom, the co-owner of several businesses in Cook County, including Voyageur

Brewing Company in Grand Marais and Voyageur Canoe Outfitters at the end of the Gunflint. Along with her husband, Mike, the Proms have outfitted trips to Quetico through Cache Bay since 1993. The Proms are also highly involved in both the Gunflint and Grand Marais communities, their faces among the most recognizable in the region. Despite Sue's standing in the community, she said that the well-known Quetico Ranger's reputation made her nervous to meet Matichuk for the first time.

"Ingela was having a birthday party for her mom and I remember being super scared to meet her," Prom confessed about her first meeting with Matichuk. "I knew she was smart, strong, and brave, and I was intimidated."

It did not take long, however, for Prom and Matichuk to realize how much they had in common. Both women raised two children, a boy and a girl, in the Northwoods. They shared a complete respect for the natural world. And furthermore, each were staggeringly hard workers. For decades, twelve-hour workdays were commonplace for them, stopping only because of darkness or other natural limitations, rarely due to simply running out of steam. Nonetheless, and contextualized by her own zeal for hard work, Prom told me she stands in awe thinking back on what Matichuk did at Cache Bay. "Her work ethic and her professional standing has remained ever steady. She is just as dedicated to Quetico Park today as she was when I first met her," Prom declared. "She has always wanted what is best for Quetico and its users. I don't think she could separate Cache Bay from her identity because it is so much of who she is. Janice is Cache Bay. Her care of the park for all of these years has made her corner of Quetico the wonderful place it is."

Deb Mark, another business owner operating near the end of the Gunflint, first crossed paths with Matichuk in the summer of 1985. She had been connected to the Gunflint scene for many decades, growing up on the Gunflint Trail and navigating both the remote business world in this pocket of Minnesota and the social dynamics of the area. She has watched U.S. Forest Service Rangers come and go throughout the BWCA and broader Superior National Forest in which it lies. For her, it is fairly easy to tell people who are a good fit for the region from those who are simultaneously on duty and fixated on their next stop. When it comes to Matichuk, Mark said the longer she stayed, the more the Cache Bay ranger's roots extended.

"Cache Bay is home to her; it is in her blood and soul," Mark said. "I couldn't imagine Janice not being in Cache Bay."

Both Deb Mark and Sue Prom first shared their reflections with me before their friend Janice was diagnosed with terminal brain cancer. Still, their sentiments ring true. It will be impossible for many to not associate Cache Bay with Janice Matichuk. I imagine that, very much in the same fashion that many canoeists remember tales of Dorothy Molter and her root beer while paddling past her island on Knife

Lake, so too will visitors think of Matichuk as they enter Quetico through Cache Bay.

Molter was once referred to as "the loneliest woman in America" in an article that ran in the *New York Times*. She lived for 56 years on Knife Lake, most of it alone, and by all accounts, preferred it that way. Many who long for solitude do. It's one thing, though, to live in civilization, pining for aloneness, and another to live it. There is now a museum in Ely, Minnesota in her honor. Bottles of root beer with her image emblazoned on the label can be found in gas stations and grocery stores throughout the Upper Midwest. Matichuk is not likely destined for such memorabilia, though if a likeness were one day erected to cement her legacy, one would hope it could hold a candle to her hard work, courage, and perseverance. Indeed, it is these traits that time and time again I heard when I asked her acquaintances to describe her approach to life as a park ranger, as a mother, and as a community member. "She's dedicated; it's as simple as that," Mark said. Indeed it is.

It is understandable that Matichuk's work ethic will be the most likely memory when her name is mentioned around Saganaga, Gunflint, and Quetico campfires. Still, no matter how dedicated one is to their profession, craft, family, or home, all work and no play is a recipe for burn-out or disaster. And despite her occasional tendency toward reclusiveness, Matichuk is an example of this reality.

If it weren't for her ability to find play through

passion for sound, movement, and their collision, manifested as dance, who knows how long she would have held it together. One cannot always be serious, cannot always be *on*.

Accordion music always had a special place in Matichuk's heart, but it is not often recognized for packing the dancefloors any longer, at least not in northeastern Minnesota or the far reaches of Ontario. Either way, to get her moving, Matichuk preferred the sound of bluegrass or rock 'n roll. "When I hear the right music, I can dance all night," Matichuk said.

She once described to me her favorite settings in which to engage in *the art of dance*. Preeminent is the North House Folk School in Grand Marais. A collection of traditionally-constructed wooden buildings adjacent to a small harbor on Lake Superior, it is an artists' hub, ground zero for creativity in the quaint lakeside town, standing out for events celebrating everything from summer solstice to acoustic music. The school brings students and instructors from all over the world, offering classes in a variety of outdoor and artistic pursuits that include everything from the heritage practice of building all-wood canoes, to more practical applications such as chainsaw safety. Matichuk was a regular of the school's contra dances throughout the summer months, and when she wasn't practicing movement in this most high-minded setting, she was just as likely to be spotted on any old tavern dance floor.

"I love dancing, oh my God... I love dancing," Matichuk said with a laugh. "That is one thing I do in town as often as I can. Either just on my own or with a gaggle of women just letting our hair down and swinging it all around."

Though an eventual favorite of hers, Matichuk knew nothing of the small town until she visited Grand Marais in 1987. In those days, Grand Marais was a much different community than the bustling tourist destination that it is in 2020. The town was still finding its way in the post-logging, post-fishing booms that literally put it on the map more than a century ago. "In the first bunch of years, I would come once a summer and that was it," Janice said of discovering Grand Marais. "North House Folk School was not there. Most of these restaurants were not there. It was an entirely different town."

The streets of downtown Grand Marais are now lined with retail shops, locally-owned restaurants, and dozens of lodgings, and a large municipal campground. It's become a landing spot for artists and outdoor enthusiasts of all ages. Some stay for a few years before rambling on, while others put down roots in the community. Prom noted how well Matichuk's artistic interests fit with the vibe and art scene in Grand Marais, harmonious with the way her passion for the wilderness is befitting of the culture within the border lakes communities. "Janice is an amazing woman who likes to dance and have fun, make no mistake," Prom said. "She is willing to try new things and be spontaneous, yet she is super dependable. She has that rugged side, but she has this deeply caring side to her as well."

In 2009, Prom organized an event that recognized Matichuk's 25 years of service at Cache Bay and Quetico Provincial Park. To the crowd gathered at a boat landing near the Chik-Wauk Museum at the end of the Gunflint Trail, Prom said of Matichuk, "She has fought forest fires, rescued capsized canoeists, and has saved lives over the years. Not just the lives of those that almost drowned, but also those who she prevented from entering life-threatening situations through her education of each and every camper that goes through Cache Bay."

Through all the trips to Grand Marais, all the winters back home in Atikokan, each season coming and going from the park, Matichuk was an individual that led many lives within a calendar year. Matichuk was the same person, at least in the physical sense, whether she was saving a life in Cache Bay or channel surfing in the dark on a cold February afternoon. Matichuk could be hailed as a national hero one day, and the next, the door closes, the lights go off, darkness arrives. Through this darkness, a light will always remain there in Cache Bay, her beacon. Countless stories ultimately make up the legend of Matichuk's life, and out of them, Quetico and the Cache Bay Ranger Station are the ultimate commonality, the centerpiece that leads every end back to its beginning.

During the reception recognizing Matichuk's exceptional service, Prom said of her friend, "Janice doesn't just educate folks; she instills a love and respect of the wilderness in everyone she meets. Her passion has reached many because wilderness has no bounds. The job as Cache Bay Ranger isn't really work for her. It's who she is. Janice's life and purpose are Quetico Park."

Chapter Seven
Quetico: The Magic Waters

On a sunny summer afternoon in 1986, Janice Matichuk was about to give up. She had paddled thirty-some miles in a day and a half, venturing far to the southwest of Cache Bay and the comfort of her ranger station. The strenuous paddle took her past large granite cliffs, several waterfalls, and all varieties of flora and fauna. Having spent most of her childhood far to the north of her station, this route's journey west was, in a way, familiar to her. At the same time, everything felt wonderfully new. There were more berries on the bushes and vines here, deeper waters, healthier forests. Stands of 200-year-old pines stretched toward the sun, having escaped from the clutches of loggers that had encroached on the other borders of the park.

This was her second season working at the Cache Bay Ranger Station and a day off in June was a rarity, so Matichuk embraced the opportunity to explore her gigantic natural neighborhood. She was on a mission this particular trip and it powered her every stroke. The ranger was out to find one of the rarest plant species in Quetico: encrusted saxifrage.

Spotting it is a treasured experience among enthusiasts, difficult to find because it grows primarily on the rugged cliffs that line the border lakes. The flower's white petals, yellow interior, and red center make it uniquely breathtaking upon inspection, and yet, even more than its beauty, those who spot the flower are enthralled simply by its scarcity. Thus, it is beautiful not solely by its elegance, but also through the reverence of persistence. Admirers look in awe, much the same as that given to alpine monks high in the Himalayas for an unwavering dedication few could put sufficient words to, let alone accurately imitate.

After completing the outgoing half of the "Man Chain Loop," a common Quetico paddling route named for its inclusion of This Man, That Man, No Man, and Other Man lakes, Matichuk was feeling disheartened. She simply could not find a single specimen of the plant that she was in search of. Her last hope was to take advantage of the intel shared with her just days before by two Quetico staffers — Naturalist Shan Walshe and Historian Shirley Peruniak. They had discovered a location of the plant and Janice had high hopes that she could find the rare plant growing there. "I scoured the cliff face in Emerald Lake from the canoe and was just about to give up, when all of a sudden, there it was," Matichuk recalled. "This rare and fragile plant clinging to what appeared to be bare rock — hard, fractured granite, the Canadian pre-Cambrian shield exposed. I was tickled pink to be allowed to see it."

And then she wept.

"Sometimes the beauty of this place just hits you," Matichuk told me, resting her palm on her jaw, deep in thought. It was not often that Matichuk was short on words, but when she did go silent, it was obvious that she was retracing memories in her mind.

The pause lasted longer than the duration of a five-rod portage before she continued. "There's something about Quetico; you have to be here to know it. You have to smell all those smells in the morning or those on a hot afternoon. You have to see these dark skies when a storm is rolling in. You have to hear all the birds and get to know the afternoon winds. You have to spend a lot of time watching, listening, smelling, and feeling. That is how you get to know the park. At least that was the case for me over all these years. I was always learning. And all the way up to my last day in the park, I will always be learning about this place."

After all this time, if I've learned anything from Janice about Quetico Provincial Park, it is that it is a place for experiences. People come from all around the world to paddle these waters. They come for lake trout, moose, wolves, bears, and the seemingly boundless waters. On the surface, many will mention *solitude* or *adventure* as the reasons that they are willing to travel such great distances to visit the park. Really, though, and perhaps unknowingly, what people seek from Quetico are experiences. Primal living that is the basis of real, good stories. It is the unknown that captures one's spirit, the wonder of how legends take form. Indeed, a trip to Quetico can yield many possibilities, including joy and despair, perfection and roughness, life and death. It's a place unlike most every other on the planet, and its history is as complex and moving as the water droplets that flow in immeasurable directions.

Travel back in time to the Pleistocene and one would observe Quetico—along with much of central North America—covered by an enormous sheet of ice. At the time, it was barren, uninviting, and yet to blossom with its natural mystique. Sustained life within the bounds of what is now Quetico arrived only as the glacier began its retreat some 20,000 years ago. Woolly mammoths and beavers the size of bears roamed the landscape, as did vicious predators like the saber-toothed tiger. At the time, a cedar canoe would have proved useless in Quetico, that is, except to be burned for a fire.

Fast forward halfway to modern day and this same region had begun to bloom into a lush landscape full of deep lakes, wild rivers, and dense forest. The first human inhabitants to walk these lands, paddle the waters, and call it home were the Paleo-Indians. Evidence suggests that they spent time in places around the border lake such as Knife Lake more than 10,000 years ago. Some of the descendants of this prehistoric migration, including Ontario's First Nations communities, have had roots here since.

This was a time of unmatched connection to the natural world for humans. From then until relative modernity, the native communities hunted, fished, and survived on these lands. It's worth noting that the park looks nearly identical to how it appeared in the 1400s. As peoples new to the Western Hemisphere began to settle in the area in the most recent millennia, the area around the parks changed greatly. Before settlement from the east was a time when birchbark canoes were not made for sport and hobby in a garage. The First Nations peoples' stories are of survival, of working the land and its abundant resources as everyday tools. These gifts were a means to travel, eat, and stay warm. The wild was everything, and while the territory is composed of lands sacred to the First Nations communities, there are also stories of pain, abandonment, and hunger here. The history of human settlement is scattered with atrocities, and the setting here in northwest Ontario's abundant natural beauty and landscape is no exception.

As the age in which the native communities celebrated life and land here began to wane, the Quetico-Superior region also served as a corridor for early European explorers and fur traders. The iconic Voyageur Highway, considered one of the main thoroughfares during that age of ruggedness and discovery, went through the heart of the border lakes. While the giant beavers of old were long gone, their smaller ancestors' pelts were prized all the same. Animals were pressured like never before, trapped and hunted to near extinction as settlers moved across the landscape. Soon after the fur trade came the age of extractive logging and mining. The late 1800s and early 1900s were a time of resource removal from the region. Some of the impacts of this mutilation are still noticeable today, though its memories and artifacts have largely been swallowed by thick vegetation.

Jon Nelson recalls this time period in his book *Quetico: Near to Nature's Heart.* I sat down with him on a windy afternoon near the beginning of winter. He told me that in historical terms, Quetico Provincial Park is very young, only officially established in 1913. Students of history like himself have the perspective to understand that time doesn't only move forward, it is also a mechanism for healing.

As such, it is through direct but unobtrusive movement on the land and water in the boundary waters region that people can truly feel a sense of connection to *both* the past and the present. Nelson hopes that perhaps, through this linking of time, people will also be concerned for the future of this pristine wilderness. In his writings and reflections on the park, Nelson notes that "There have been times in the Quetico—snowshoeing at dusk along the French River, ambling along the ancient sand beach at The Pines on Pickerel Lake, paddling beneath the giant pine trees on McNiece Lake, or simply sitting around the campfire in the evening—when I have profoundly felt as if I am held *in* the land, not separate and apart from it."

For her part, Matichuk was not much of a historian, though well enough versed in the park's past. Most of her stories were not deep reflections on what the park was like fifty, seventy-five, or hundreds of years ago. Her tales are less grand, both by their setting in a moment and in their gravity relative to the context of the park's history. For Matichuk, life unfolded in tiny increments. Each bird that visited the trees on her island was a story. Each canoeist who passed through was worth hearing from. Every day, a stand-alone chapter in the book of Matichuk.

"I like to know the history of this place," Matichuk told me. "It makes for educated conversation. It provides a better way of thinking about where you are. I also like hearing about where a canoe camper is from. What their story is. What brought them here to the park. It's all part of the history of this place, each journey that passes through Cache Bay."

Andrea Allison, a recently retired librarian, spent many years working at the Quetico headquarters on French Lake. Allison has long been an admirer of Matichuk and her dedication to the park, going so far as to nominate the Cache Bay Ranger for the Ministry of Natural Resources PRIDE Service Award in 1998. "Janice is very, very dedicated to her job," Allison said. "She loves Cache Bay and it's important to her that visitors receive the best information she can give them in terms of safety, orientation to the park, points of interest, history of the park, things like that."

People who sign up to be park rangers are inclined to explore the terrain in some capacity. Fresh hires at Yellowstone or Glacier National Parks, for example, are bound to take to the trails at some point, regardless of their ambition or skill set in the backcountry. With Matichuk, however, her approach was different right from the beginning. Nobody demanded, or even requested, that she explore her new realm. A natural pull led Matichuk to the woods, and a desire to be educated on that of which she spoke when she issued permits to enter the park. Allison recalls that, during Matichuk's first few years working at the Cache Bay Ranger Station, "She made every effort to explore the park so she could give visitors to Quetico firsthand information on sites to see and hazards to be aware of, particularly in the Falls Chain area."

Matichuk and Allison shared a canoe at various times while they were employed by Quetico, with the latter settling into retirement before the former was willing to mention the word. It was on these outings that Allison realized how much love and passion Matichuk truly had for Quetico. "She views it as her home, not just as a place where she works," Allison said. "We paddled to where Benny Ambrose lived on Ottertrack one time. Another time, she showed me the pictograph site in Cache Bay. She went to these places because she was interested in people, the history of Quetico, and Janice wanted to know *everything* she could about the park."

Another longtime friend and colleague in the park, Karen Mikoliew, echoes Allison's sentiments. A former Quetico interior warden, Mikoliew said Matichuk considered Quetico's woods and waters to be much more than mere physical landscapes or features. Mikoliew praised Matichuk's ability to embrace a metaphysical relationship with the park. Through this lens, Quetico was a mindset, not just a place. "Janice believes in the idealism that is Quetico," Mikoliew explained. "She understands its worth as a living ecosystem so that the world's people have a piece of nature to come and enjoy."

Mikoliew's first job in the park was for the 1989 season as a park warden stationed in Cache Bay. At that time, the island adjacent to Janice's had cabins for portage maintenance crews, though they have since been removed to emphasize a more natural feel at the park's entrance. Mikoliew remembers meeting Matichuk and becoming instantly intrigued by her curiosity and passion. "Sometimes I would think that Janice was dedicated almost to a fault," she said. "It's this insatiable curiosity for all things, from bush planes to nature. She was just always trying, each day it seemed, to get a better understanding of the Quetico community and its history."

After that first summer, Mikoliew went on to be an interior warden for 13 more seasons. Her patrol area brought her through the Cache Bay district regularly, and it remained one of her favorite areas in the 1.2-million-acre park, mainly due to Matichuk.

"She's tougher than nails," Mikoliew said of Janice with an obvious sense of pride. "She can do anything."

While we talked one afternoon, sitting on a jagged stretch of Lake Superior shoreline, Matichuk recalled anecdotes of the campers she had met throughout her decades at Cache Bay. It was a calm day on Superior this time, the sound of intermittent traffic from nearby Highway 61 heard in the absence of crashing waves and rolling stones. Matichuk told me that the type of people who are drawn to Quetico are not always who one might think. Over the past three decades, Matichuk has issued permits to doctors from the Mayo Clinic, businesswomen from California, and lawyers from Minneapolis.

"People get the idea it's always old white guys with grey hair who paddle through here," she said. "And sure, they're here. They come through. But we have people of all ages, from all 50 states, different countries, men, women, and children every year that come to my island."

There is, however, one critical piece of variation that is lacking. Most paddlers on both sides of the border are white. A common issue across most types of outdoor recreation throughout North America, this narrowness is not unique to the paddling community. Most downhill skiers, cyclists, and indeed, canoeists, are white. As Matichuk and I talked about the future of the boundary waters and what it might look like in 20, 50, or even 100 years, we talked about people of color and how to present the park in a more accessible way.

It is obvious that without more buy-in from a broader coalition, the wilderness, especially south of the border, is under threat. The survival of these places in their current state is certainly dependent on getting more people exposed. After all, one cannot love what one does not know. But that exposure necessarily requires the education that is delivered by people like Matichuk during permit pick-up, at least if preservation is a priority. On this issue, a distinction must be made between the two parks.

Quetico is not marketed in the same fashion as its counterpart across the international border. Quetico is meant to be a protected wilderness, not necessarily a playground. It is first and foremost a preserve and secondarily a recreation area. The Boundary Waters Canoe Area may be the inverse. Amid the COVID-19 pandemic and 2020 civil unrest, many new faces entered the woods. They sought a respite from the chaos in one of the premier places to find it. Unfortunately, the context of this influx of people lessened the degree of good that was done by such exposure. Mandatory education during permit pickup was relaxed and heavy use of the wilderness area brought reports of campsites being trashed and the land disrespected. Leave No Trace ethics could not be found. On the other side of the imaginary line that separates them, Quetico is a different place than the BWCA. Campsites have less amenities, no wall-less latrine in the woods, no campfire grate. It is less accessible by design. It could be argued that this philosophy, the requirement to *rough it* to an even greater degree, does a better job at delivering the solace that is the ultimate goal of these places. Lovers of wilderness take note.

Nelson, the writer, historian, and former Quetico staffer, was born in Minnesota and later became a dual citizen of Canada and the United

States. It was the remoteness of Quetico that first pulled him across the border decades ago, though he told me in 2019 that the state of American politics made his move appear clairvoyant. To his credit, Nelson has likely spent more time documenting and researching the history of Quetico than nearly any other person in history. That is, perhaps, with one exception: Shirley Peruniak.

Born in 1926 on the east side of Algonquin Provincial Park near the Canadian capital, Ottawa, Peruniak headed west, working as a naturalist in Quetico for decades. She was awarded the prestigious Order of Ontario award for her dedication to preserving the history of the region. Her book, *Quetico Provincial Park: An Illustrated History,* is the perfect complement to Nelson's written history and extensive research. Peruniak, too, spent hundreds, or even thousands of hours learning the history of the park firsthand. "I talked to trappers, park rangers, poachers, and elders from the Lac LaCroix First Nations, anyone who knew about where the park had come from," Peruniak said in a 2010 interview with the *Frontenac News,* a community newspaper from her hometown of Shabot Lake. "I remember getting children to interview their grandparents, who only spoke Ojibwe, and having them translate for me."

Nelson said that Peruniak had a natural way of extracting information and stories from people, and her list of interviewees stretched back to some of the first rangers to work in Quetico. In a reflection he wrote in 2010, Nelson recalled that people told their firsthand recollections to Peruniak. Though natural and wild back then, practices were a bit different. She talked to people "about using dynamite to shorten portages and about guiding celebrities like Mae West and Charles Lindbergh into the park."

Matichuk cited to me not just Peruniak's natural knowledge, having steered her toward rare plants during her first years in the park, but also her kindness, only having fond memories of the longtime Quetico advocate. When Peruniak passed away in January 2020 at the age of 93, I asked Janice what first came to mind about her old friend. The first thing she recalled were the legendary "Shirley Cookies" that she often carried in a small daypack, and the joy they brought to paddlers and park staff of all ages. The homemade creations were a twist of the standard chocolate chip cookie. Peruniak's blend featured additional ingredients, including dried fruit, walnuts, and a sugary blast from gooey gumdrops. According to Matichuk, the cookies were handy for Peruniak as she went about collecting stories and trying to get people to open up about the history of the region and its connection to them.

"Shirley, like a lot of us, considered Quetico to be the single greatest canoe park in the world," Matichuk said.

Ranking Quetico as the best park to put a canoe in is a notion that many find hard to dispute. Less stringent regulations in Minnesota's BWCA can mean more traffic in the backcountry. The woods and waters of Quetico are kept additionally quiet by a moderately higher cost to access than that of the Boundary Waters. In Quetico, there is a per-night, per-person camping fee charged to visitors. This adds up when contrasted to the one-time, unlimited night permit that visitors to the BWCA must carry. It is also far more complicated for a U.S. citizen to enter Quetico than it is the BWCA, namely because trips that cross the border by hull and paddle require anyone over the age of 18 to get prior approval to do so. This Remote Area Border Crossing Permit, or RABCP, has its own fees on top of the nightly fees to be in the park. When given the choice between the simplicity and cost of a BWCA trip and a Quetico trip, for many, the BWCA wins out.

That's not to say, though, that even if more paddlers from south of the border wanted to choose Quetico, they could. The park is managed much more restrictedly in order to protect the land, and park managers do not allow nearly the volume that the BWCA sees annually. Approximately 200,000 people enter the BWCA on any given year, making it the most visited wilderness area in the nation. Meanwhile, Quetico averages 20,000 visitors per year.

"The campers who come through Quetico say they are willing to come here and pay our fees because of the way we manage it," Matichuk said. "They tell us they come here because they get to have this deep experience with the land and water without the crowds."

It isn't hard to find examples of that deep experience if you know where to look. Canoe builder and longtime Quetico paddler, Ken Koscik, recalled crossing paths with a group of four anxious young men from Chicago while checking in at the Cache Bay Ranger Station. The four, all firefighters for the city of Chicago, stood in front of Matichuk as she described the various safety protocols and rules for traveling inside the park. "They weren't listening and were acting like they knew it all," Koscik said. They wanted to go catch fish and had little time for the ranger's instructions and guidance. A week later, as Koscik and his paddling crew exited the park back through Cache Bay, Matichuk informed them that the firefighters had also returned that morning.

"Janice said each one of those four men stood in her office talking and talking about all the butterflies they saw, the moose, the waterfalls, the stars, and how amazing every little detail of their trip was," Koscik said. "She said she finally had to explain to them that she had to get back to a project outside the ranger station so they'd get to moving on. That's what this place does to people. It slows them down for a little bit. There's a calming effect that the park has on people."

While those firefighters certainly found butterflies and daisies, they also found time for their original goal. Janice confessed to me that though she had never been quite as enamored with the pursuit, fishing remains a very popular activity in canoe country. Walleye, northern pike, smallmouth bass, and lake trout are the targets for most anglers around here. Though some paddlers don't even carry a rod and reel, many others are preoccupied almost exclusively by where and when the fish are biting. The longtime ranger was not likely to offer the typical nuggets of information that aspiring anglers are used to.

"I'm not fussy about being asked, 'How's the fishing?'" Matichuk said, though her shoulders tightened and her eyes grew apprehensive when I broached the subject. "When people ask how the fishing is, I ask them right back, 'How are you as a fisherman?'"

Most reply with a general response—"decent," or, "so-so"—to which Matichuk would inform them of her fishing philosophy: the fishing is equal to and no greater than your skills as an angler. "If they tell me they're average fishermen, I let them know the fishing is average," she explained. "If they're confident about what to do, the fishing is probably going to be pretty good. If you suck at fishing, then, hmmm, the fishing might not be so good. They have an *aha* moment and we have a laugh. It's as simple as that."

I spent several summers working at a canoe outfitter on the Gunflint Trail, about 40 miles from Cache Bay. A dedicated and perhaps obsessive angler, I was continually amazed at the number of people who came to the boundary waters and hadn't thought much about fishing. They went for the paddling, and as it turned out, fishing was an afterthought, if included on their itinerary at all. Groups of venturers would return from a trip to the BWCA and boast of how wonderful their time had been, making no mention of fishing.

I suppose if one sets out solely to catch fish on a trip to the wilderness, it's possible they will return home disappointed. There are fish to be caught, make no mistake. It's what one might miss along that way that needs to be considered. In recent years, I have learned to blend both pursuits on my canoe trips: fishing and presence. Matichuk helped me to better understand this, that there is more to a canoe trip than bagging a limit of walleye. It's the sounds. The feeling. The water. Gathering around the warmth of the fire to talk with friends. "Have your fun fishing, that's great," Matichuk told me. "But don't forget that there's so much more happening out here. Keep your ears and eyes open. And keep your mind open."

Despite her disinterest in fishing relative to many others, she recognized that more people fishing meant a more certain future for places like this. In her final decade, the numbers of anglers each season had reached a bit of a lull. One particularly busy summer long ago, before the licenses were generated and printed electronically, Matichuk developed a mild case of carpal tunnel syndrome from writing out so many licenses and permits. "It used to be common to unlock the door to the ranger station at 7 or 8 a.m. and see a group of campers coming in from afar, just standing there, drooling, waiting to go in and catch fish," Matichuk said. "We just don't see that like we used to."

In those long and short thirty-five years, Janice

Matichuk saw all kinds. She knew many of the more than 2,000 campsites in Quetico, more often empty than not. On any given night, even during the peak of the paddling season, no more than 200 of those sites are likely to be occupied. Much of her time in Quetico existed in an otherworldly quiet; others, it was eardrum-rattling loud. Wind, fire, thunderstorms, and other natural disruptions are part of what makes Quetico the vibrant landscape it is. Whether fishing, trapping, wilderness survival, or simply passing through, for centuries, humans have been only a piece of this diverse ecosystem. Matichuk understood our role here. Perhaps that was why she wasn't too impressed with her title as the "longest serving interior ranger in the history of Quetico."

"It's a nice thing to think about," she said. "I'm just now getting to a spot where I can look back on everything that's happened to me out here and let it sink in a little bit. But there's so much that happened before me, so many people who were here before I was even a thought in the history of this place."

That might be the case, and indeed there is a rich history to these lands and waters, complex like the ranger herself. The park's story is something Nelson, Peruniak, and a select few others have dedicated significant portions of their lives to documenting. For Matichuk, she might have thought her story was but a footnote in the overall legend of this land. All the same, former Quetico Superintendent Dave Elder made it clear to me the gravity of what Matichuk experienced during the time on her island.

"Janice has given everything to this island," he said, "for a period of time that no one else will ever equal."

Chapter Eight
A Cloak of Darkness

"It would be hard for me now, at this age and stage, to leave a song without a glimmer of hope... I always like to have a glimmer of hopefulness, even in collapse."
—**Gord Downie, Canadian singer-songwriter, musician, writer, and activist who died from brain cancer in October 2017**

It wasn't supposed to end this way. Not for Janice Matichuk. Not for her story. In an instant, cancer changed everything. It impacts so many families, futures, and best-laid plans. She called on a Sunday afternoon with the news. I picked up the phone. She got right to it.

"I have brain cancer," she said.

The skies continued to darken, a dazzling summer blue hours before. I sat there listening, clumsily clutching my phone. Some much-needed rain had been in the forecast and it was moving in as predicted. The forest in northeastern Minnesota was desert dry. Leaves from living birch trees were starting to drop, strangled by the lack of precipitation that the summer had provided. Thunder rumbled towards me from the horizon as I watched large poplar trees creak back and forth, harbingers of the approaching storm. It was June 14, 2020.

I said very little, just listening to Janice explain what the diagnosis meant. It was quite simple, really—the tumor growing in her brain was going to kill her. Both the phone call and the news that came from it was out of nowhere. My friend was fine one day, dying the next. There was no reason to think she was ill, let alone terminally so. The previous year had been one of Janice's hardest. Her 2019 season was cut short when she lost her finger in August; then the already-protracted off-season was extended, this time by the pandemic, the 2020 season opener delayed. But the recovery effort was, by June and by all accounts, going quite well, and Matichuk was back in the park. The rest of her life played out tragically fast, working in Quetico on the Saturday one week before she called me, and essentially retired from the park by the time she broke the news.

Janice and I hadn't communicated on a regular basis during the previous six weeks before the phone call other than a few short back-and-forth emails. The border separating the U.S. and Canada remained closed as the worldwide pandemic surged along. It was also a time of great unrest in Minnesota, what with protests and riots in Minneapolis, an intense spotlight shone upon our state. A black man, George Floyd, had been killed by police officers in broad daylight and with cameras rolling just weeks before.

Reactions throughout the country were swift. The world roiled with tension. The border country never seemed so far apart.

And then, cancer. Janice Matichuk had brain cancer. Glioblastoma, to be exact. A search of that word took me to the Mayo Clinic website where I learned that most people who are diagnosed with it die within a year. Surgery is an option in some cases, though it's typically nothing more than an expensive and painful way to buy a little more time. When successful, that additional time that surgery provides gives loved ones a chance to create a few extra, final memories. When it isn't, an already horrible situation becomes worse; when operating on the brain, the ultimate risk is a permanent loss of the ability to communicate. Matichuk had options. None of them were worth considering.

"It's got me scared," Matichuk repeatedly told me as we talked about her diagnosis.

Janice and I talked for about 20 minutes. She cried several times; I felt the need to choke mine back. When I found out my grandfather died, I remember feeling the same, bottling up the tears as my mind spun. I'm sure Sherri Moe and others in her field would have an explanation for that. Scientific facts and rigorous analysis of the human brain are wonderful tools for better understanding our emotions, but as I listened to Janice, I had no concern for reasoning or logic. I wanted Matichuk's pain to hurt me only on the inside, not the out. I succeeded in that. Grief crushed me, it was a mountain of solid granite.

The conversation came to its natural conclusion and I hung up the phone. A small squirrel danced across a downed balsam fir out my westerly window. It paused when it neared the top of the fallen tree, nervously surveying its options, before darting off into the distant timber. I closed my eyes as the deafening silence made way for rain, droplets pelting the roof of my small cabin. Finally, the rain was here. Our forests could drink. Life would be nourished. After weeks of absence, I realized how much I missed its sound. There was nothing else to be done. I sat and was present, just as Janice had taught me.

For months, Janice and I had been planning to meet again at Cache Bay, sometime in late May or early June. Everything was lined up; we just needed to get there. The idea was that Mark Hargis, one of the men Matichuk saved 20 years prior, would meet up with the two of us to commemorate the passing of his friend, Tom Ackerman. It was going to be the first time Hargis had returned to Cache Bay since the day Ackerman died. Instead, the border closure because of the uncontained coronavirus was repeatedly extended, our targeted meeting date pushed back further and further into the summer.

I shared Matichuk's circumstances with Hargis about a week after I first learned of them. In an email, I told him that Janice was sick, that her time at Cache Bay was likely coming to an end. The commemorative trip, initially postponed, was now off the table, its cornerstone party member now withdrawn.

Hargis took a few days to get back to me. I could wait. Hargis might need space to process the sudden turn of events, I understood. When we connected, we were raw. Ackerman had died almost 20 years to the day. And now Janice, the park ranger who was credited by Hargis, his brother, uncle, and cousins with saving their lives, was dying, distant closure denied. Nothing about the situation was easy. "My feelings are a bit of sadness and sorrow," Hargis told me. "It would have been great just to express our gratitude to her for saving our lives, and to fill her in on the impact we each are making on a daily basis."

Photographs of Hargis from the time since that day in Cache Bay show a classic, all-American life. Along with his wife, Jennie, Hargis is often smiling ear-to-ear, their young children at their sides. He showed me photos of them at Target Field, the home baseball stadium of the Minnesota Twins, as well as the family in Disneyland, traveling abroad with Jennie, and spending casual afternoons on the golf course. Not one picture in the collection was of Hargis in a canoe or recreating on the water.

Mark did return to the Gunflint Trail several times in the course of the past 20 years. He went as far as to travel to the end of the Gunflint and mighty Sag in 2013. As we planned our rendezvous, Hargis told me he wanted to "Revisit Sag as an opportunity to overcome some of the anxiety with canoeing and water." In his previous attempt, Sag had denied him this relief, the lake in no mood for such peace. The waters were again dashed with white caps, high winds, and dark clouds rolling in, an ominous echo of his past there. He quickly abandoned the mission that day, retreating to shore before he got close to the spot where Ackerman died all that time ago. "Being on Sag that day was as scary as the day Tom drowned," Hargis said.

Still, Hargis seemed committed, passionate even, about meeting Matichuk and me at Cache Bay in the summer of 2020. Matichuk's presence was, no doubt, the missing element. If there was a soul on earth to help vanquish Mark's trauma, it was her. However difficult the process of visiting the site would have been for Hargis— perhaps Matichuk as well—the push to do so had been together.

Making peace with the passing of a loved one, let alone when it is unexpected and too soon, does not come easy. Death is certainly part of the great, harmonious cycle, but those lost are no less missed. Hargis knows this all too well. Though faith has helped him find meaning in the constant struggle that is life, Ackerman's death continues to affect Hargis. "I have fought for closure, but this experience is something that I think about each and every day. I don't think there can be closure to an event that impacts our lives in such a drastic manner," Hargis said. "I think events like that become a big part of the fabric of who we are and who we become after."

Loss is simultaneously easier and more difficult by its prevalence. On one hand, it is comfortable to relate. On the other, it refreshes one's pain. Matichuk's brain cancer was just so. Mark's father, Bill, died in 2018, also from brain cancer, just 68 at the time of his death. Bill Hargis remains a widely recognizable name in Minnesota's Twin Cities Metro. He served as the mayor of Woodbury from 1993 to 2010, fostering the community's doubling in size while the vine of urban sprawl grew south and east from Minneapolis and St. Paul. According to his obituary in the *St. Paul Pioneer Press*, Woodbury honored Bill by naming a street after him—Hargis Parkway, a road that runs past a local high school.

Mark told me, "The last four months that we had with our dad were some of the hardest days of my life." Having endured the same affliction as Matichuk's first-hand, Mark's empathy stretched most mightily to Janice's children, Ingela and Leif. It was clear that what they were going through was weighing heavily upon his mind. "I really feel for her and her family," Hargis said. "The pain of watching your loved one struggle and die is very difficult." The pain he felt for his father now transformed into pain for them.

In the middle of July 2020, Matichuk and I connected once again. The mood was much lighter than the previous time we had spoken. Janice sounded much more like—Janice. It was the mention of her children that caused the most reflection in me. Matichuk spoke proudly about how Ingela and Leif were handling her affliction.

There was despair, Janice said, particularly for Leif. Not long after the initial diagnosis, there was a moment when he broke down. He and Janice were driving back to Atikokan from Thunder Bay when Leif suddenly had to pull over. "He fell to pieces and started to sob so hard that he was shaking," Matichuk said.

Throughout that time, however, both Leif and Ingela remained steadfast by their mother's side. By no means did any of them wallow in despair. They organized a camping trip to an island where Janice often went with her own parents and brothers when she was little. Ingela participated in a virtual event, a long walk to raise awareness for brain cancer, and spent hours researching natural methods to ease the suffering caused by the disease that was taking over her mother's body. Each were at their mother's side whenever she needed them. "Time to make mom my full-time job, no matter the cost, just like she did raising us," Ingela said in a post online on June 30th.

For her part, Matichuk never mentioned or even alluded to *giving up*. She was well aware of the physical strength she possessed. On several occasions after the cancer diagnosis came in, Matichuk referenced her amputated index finger. She told me that while she lay in her uniform in the hospital bed, nearly unconscious from a lack of sleep and a day of immense pain, her strength never wavered. She believed at that time that she could and would make it through the accident. It did work again, as did she, but never again back at Cache Bay. "Nobody thought that finger would go back on, let alone work again," she boasted. "I proved them all wrong."

The latter part of her statement still gives me

pause. It was interesting, coming from Matichuk. In the nearly three years I spent with her, she never once mentioned doing something to *prove someone wrong*. Invariably thinking of others first, if Matichuk had a flaw, it was that her gentleness hid her strength. She did not try to rattle naysayers who said a woman had no place in a logging camp. Her pride was not in being a woman who worked at the Cache Bay Ranger Station; it was simply having worked at the Cache Bay Ranger Station. She did not spend most of her life working in Quetico to become an icon of the North Woods, though certainly she did create this image as a result.

To try to identify *it* is an act of futility. No list could define her. Hard work and deconstructed social norms are inadequate. Sue Prom emphasized this fact to me. That there was more to Matichuk than her legacy inside the park and the decades she spent on the island. Janice was more than someone who could split wood with an axe in her mid-60s better than most men in their 30s. She was more than a park ranger. She was more than a hard worker. "People forget or maybe don't know that Janice has amazing talent as an artist," Prom said. "She's a wealth of knowledge, yes, but also selfless, giving, and a great listener. Janice has too many positive qualities to list them all."

In the end, all of our friends, loved ones, and even our heroes face the same fate. For Janice, that too was true. She died the night of August 4th, 2020. Janice went peacefully in her sleep at home in Atikokan. Her brother, Darcy, and their father, Sam, were both able to visit Janice on her last day. As she took her final breaths, Ingela and Leif were both nearby. "My mother spent her last days listening to her favorite music, smelling the fresh air and her favorite scents, and even had a campfire in her backyard, loved ones by her side," Ingela said.

Though hundreds of learned and green visitors alike have paddled through Cache Bay in the time since Janice's passing, for many, the memories there will remain unchanged. In 2018, dedicated Quetico paddler Ken Koscik surpassed his 50th consecutive year of paddling in the park, collecting an actual lifetime's worth of memories during these trips. And yet, when I asked him to list his favorites, the memories were not of those things one would expect: the wildlife, deep forests, solitude, or wild weather. They were of Janice, and they were simple.

"One of my favorite days in the park was on a cold, wet, just miserable day," Koscik said. "We stopped in at the ranger station on our way there in Cache Bay and Janice put on some tea for us. It was Tetley Tea, a Canadian tea. Nothing fancy, but it was the best tea I'd ever tasted. That was such a great day, sitting there and warming up in the cabin and sharing tea with Janice. I'll never forget it."

Koscik said he's since ordered a box of Tetley Tea and it didn't taste nearly as good without the proper ingredients. "Janice told me it's the water in Cache Bay that makes a good cup of tea. She's right about that. There is something to treasure about the water there." She isn't wrong, but I have to venture a guess that it wasn't *just* the water that made the tea so perfect that day.

Matichuk's longtime friend from the Gunflint Trail, Bonnie Schudy, understands the sentiment. These are sacred waters. Schudy said she is ambivalent about how she'll feel on her first trip through Cache Bay without Matichuk there at the ranger station. "It's going to be strange. On one hand, of course I'll be excited to be going on a canoe trip to this beautiful place, but I'll know that Janice won't be there. Knowing that going in, and that she won't be coming back, and knowing all her stuff will be gone from the ranger station, it's going to be tough those first few times, and maybe forever. Very tough."

Schudy said that, throughout the summer of 2020, she would occasionally wake up in the middle of the night and think that Matichuk's cancer diagnosis was nothing more than a bad dream. "I see her right before I wake up and she is fine," Schudy told me in late July.

It is understandable that Matichuk cannot be separated from her image as the hard-working ranger, spirited in everything she publicly did. Leaders like her wear uniforms and put on a smile, even when they don't feel like it. She did for 35 years, to the best of her ability, and she did it with style.

Janice Matichuk was the ultimate badass. It's really that simple. She is the first female of note to live and work in an Ontario logging camp. She is the longest serving ranger in the history of Quetico Provincial Park. Her time at Cache Bay represents a career and legacy that will not be matched. And more than simply on the payroll, she is the Ultimate Ambassador to Quetico, as the park's serving superintendent, Trevor Gibb, described her to me.

Gibb visited her at her house in Atikokan in the week after her cancer diagnosis; never one to miss an opportunity, Matichuk offered Gibb "sage advice" on park operations, the same as she had over the many years. When I asked him for his thoughts on the future of Cache Bay and what comes next for the remote outpost following Matichuk's storied run, it was difficult for him to put into words. "It certainly is a tough time for everyone here at the park right now," Gibb said, opting to keep his sentiments brief. How could one possibly replace someone so perfectly singular?

For Hargis and the four other men Matichuk rescued on a stormy, chaotic June day, the significance of the ranger's career is not measured by longevity, but by its repercussion. Hargis, along with his brother Peter, his uncle Jeff, and his cousins Scott Black and Rob Anderson, would have almost certainly succumbed to the unforgiving waters of Saganaga Lake without Matichuk's intervention. There were no other canoes on the water that day. There was nobody else to come to their aid. The only help was Matichuk. Regardless of the imperfect outcome, the odds that Matichuk happened to be outside at the exact moment they needed her and that she heard their desperate cries over the horrendous storm are so unbelievably slim, that the result is reasonably miraculous. Mark has played the scenario over and over in his mind. It gives his life purpose to this day, something he doesn't take lightly. "To make my life *worthy* of saving," he told me, "that is my daily burden and challenge."

As Hargis and the others stood in shock and nearing hypothermia, screaming for their lives, Tom Ackerman descended to the bottom of Saganaga Lake. While his friends fought for survival in the chaos above, the waters far beneath the surface were calm, dark, and quiet. Though the image of sinking is a terrifying thought, there was perhaps a certain peace in that submissive darkness. The fight was over.

Ackerman stayed cloaked in blackness for nearly 48 hours before he was located, the five survivors long since transported back to the Gunflint Trail and the Minnesota mainland. Difficult phone calls were made to families and friends. Hargis remembers them all. He can perfectly recall the initial shock beginning to clear, his confusion turning to tears as the reality of the situation took hold. "I can still remember how they sounded, the voices on the other end of some of those phone calls," Hargis said, clearly still shaken by the news he had to deliver that day.

By the next morning, the Ontario Provincial Police and numerous park staff were at the island in Cache Bay, the operation to retrieve Ackerman's body fully underway. The two days that were spent searching for Ackerman's body presented a strange necessity for Matichuk and her son. Leif, who was in the small cabin when the five survivors staggered in, freezing and full of fear, needed closure with the situation. He knew Ackerman was out there, lost somewhere in the waters out there that were *his*. Leif spent his childhood memorizing them in the same way most kids do, staring out at their driveways or dandelion-filled backyards. While his mother was forced to maintain business on the island, Leif desperately desired to know the outcome of Ackerman and his body. His mind ran through different scenarios. Troubling images cluttered his thoughts.

Finally, near the end of the second full day, Ackerman's body was located and brought up. He was placed in a large bag that zipped down the center and taken by boat back to the dock at Cache Bay. There, Janice and Leif stood waiting. Looking back on that night, Janice said her son was holding her hand, Leif's right clutching Janice's left. Several uniformed officers from the Ontario Provincial Police, and at least two others in full wetsuits, greeted them in workmen tones following the strenuous extraction. An officer explained to Matichuk the process for returning Ackerman to the United States while Leif stood quietly next to her, still holding his mother's hand.

As the discussion wrapped up, Leif made eye contact with one of the officers for long enough to ask what the body looked like when they found it. The officer looked at Janice, paused, and then answered Leif's question.

"You know, he looked really peaceful," the

officer said.

Leif then gave his mother's hand three squeezes, a family tradition between Ingela, Leif, and Janice, a way to show that they were okay in stressful times. "I was so happy they told Leif that, explaining that the water was so clean and so cold, that the body was okay, like he was in a deep sleep. I think Leif was thinking about me being down there, to tell you the truth. He knew it was dangerous that I went out there after them that day. I think he was thinking about what it would have been like if that was me in the body bag. What it would be like if I was gone and how alone he would have felt in that moment," Janice said.

After staring across the waters of Cache Bay for more than 30 years, Matichuk came to understand better than anyone what was happening around the peninsula that serves as a natural door between her island and Sag. She knew what weather was coming based on wind direction and the smell of the air. It is her island. No one will ever know it the way she did. From 1985 until 2019, this was her domain. She protected Cache Bay. As Sue Prom put it, "Janice is Cache Bay." And yet, with or without her physical presence, the waters of Saganaga will continuously flow through the bay, a natural cycle and one full of purpose. It is this cycle that brought her here.

On brilliant July nights, when the canoe campers have moved on to their campsites and nightfall blankets the pines, she'll be there. Warm summer evenings full of stars and endless possibilities, those were the best, Janice said.

In moments like these, with the secrecy of night as her guide, she would walk to the water's edge, gracefully enter, glide onto her back, extend her arms outward, and transform from earthly being into something else, something beyond what can be understood from our limited perspective. Cloaked in darkness and floating still in the cold water, Matichuk slowed her breathing and looked up. "It was so black that I did not know the difference between the sky and the water," she said of one of these cherished moments. "I felt like I was in some type of tank, floating in a void. It was nothing but pitch black and stars. And the stars were on the water, above me and beside me. I would float on my back like that for so long and just look and look."

Before she continued her story, Matichuk paused, sighed quietly, and took a deep breath.

"I was surrounded by blackness. There were times that I thought, if I drown right now, if something happened and I went down, I would have a smile on my face. It would be okay. In those moments, I was so profoundly grateful for everything. I had such a clear understanding of what life is and how intense it is. I have had these thoughts throughout my entire life."

Acknowledgements

This book would not have happened without support from the administrative staff at Quetico Provincial Park. Great thanks to Trevor Gibb and all the Quetico employees, those still working and those who have moved on, for their support with this project.

The finished product of this book is far different than the proposal I originally submitted to Sean Bloomfield and Colton Witte at 10,000 Lakes Publishing. It's also much different than the initial draft chapters I submitted as we neared completion of the book, or at least, what we thought would be the pages of this book. The closure of the U.S. and Canada border in 2020 presented our first major obstacle in completing the manuscript. The original plan for the last chapter was to travel with Mark Hargis, Janice Matichuk, and possibly a family member of Tom Ackerman to the border waters near Cache Bay where Tom drowned in 2000. It was all lined up to return to the site June 1, 2020, exactly 20 years to the day after Tom drowned, as is written about in Chapter One of this book. The border closure made that impossible, so we adjusted our plans. Regardless, thank you to Mark for being willing to explore such an intense possibility.

The border closure due to COVID-19 dwarfed in comparison to the news of Janice's brain cancer and, ultimately, her death. Janice and I spent many, many hours talking about her life and what would eventually become this book. I have approximately 27 hours of recorded audio, indeed enough digital tape to playback for more than a full day without stopping, in addition to endless follow-up conversations and stacks of notes from our repeated correspondence. Though she was always willing to share her time, I knew I was beginning to pester her with my repeated requests for more information when she answered the phone one morning in March by saying: "Oh, it's you again." After an awkward pause, we both couldn't help but laugh.

This book was partially rewritten over the summer of 2020 to accurately reflect the news of Janice's death. It made the editing process challenging, so indeed a great thanks to Sean and Colton for allowing the time and space to make these adjustments.

Thank you to everyone who took time to share stories and reflections about Janice, most notably her children, Ingela and Leif. Their involvement in this book was key to its completion. I thank Leif for his kindness and patience. Not unlike her mother, I bombarded Ingela with repeated requests for information and insight. Without Ingela's help, this book would be a fraction of what it is.

Others who shared stories and gave their time

to talk about Janice include: Sue Prom, Deb Mark, Jim Wiinanen, Bonnie Schudy, Sherry and Dick Powell, Becky Kayser, John and Julie Rose, Francis Walsh, Sherri Moe, Tom McCann, Ken Koscik, Steve and Melinda Wagner, Chris Rudolph, Karen Mikoliew, Andrea Allison, Jon Nelson, Sam Matichuk, Dave Elder, Al Wainwright, Scott Black and Peter Hargis.

Thanks to Stu Osthoff for publishing Chapter One of this book in the winter 2019-20 edition of his magazine, the *Boundary Waters Journal*.

Thanks also to my friend and neighbor Tim Cochrane, who literally helped lay the foundation to the small writer's cabin where most of this book was written. Additional thanks to Randy Schnobrich and the team from the North House Folk School in Grand Marais for building the cabin.

My friend and creative collaborator, Matthew Baxley, shared many photographs that are used in this book. Matthew was seated at the dinner table inside the Cache Bay Ranger Station the night Janice and I first discussed writing a book about her life, focusing on her time in Quetico. It's amazing how a steak dinner, a cup of coffee afterward, and wonderful campfire conversation can transform into something like a biography.

It is with great sorrow that I won't be able to share and celebrate this book with Janice, at least not in person. I desperately want to hand her a hardcopy of this book so I can see the look on her face as she flips through the pages. In many ways, Janice wrote this book. These are all her stories. I simply listened and put the words down on paper. In crafting these pages, it feels like we designed and built a house together. It's a public house for everyone to see, or at least offer the chance to peak through the windows so as to get a better understanding of who she was. It hurts that I don't get to share it with her, as she shared so much with me. Regardless, this 'building' now stands in her honor. Thank you, Janice. We did it.

About the Author

Writer and journalist Joe Friedrichs has been reporting on environmental issues and outdoor news in the United States for more than 15 years. His writing can be found in dozens of publications throughout the country, from Montana to Minnesota. *Her Island* is his first nonfiction book.

For more information about this book, to contact the author, or to learn more about 10,000 Lakes Publishing, visit 10kLP.com. Additional 10,000 Lakes Publishing titles include:

Adventure North by Sean Bloomfield
Waters Beneath my Feet by Jerry Pushcar
Justin Cody's Race to Survival by Cliff Jacobson
The Eddy by Joe Paatalo

Made in the USA
Monee, IL
12 July 2024